A COMPANION TO THE BOOK OF REVELATION

CASCADE COMPANIONS

The Christian theological tradition provides an embarrassment of riches: from Scripture to modern scholarship, we are blessed with a vast and complex theological inheritance. And yet this feast of traditional riches is too frequently inaccessible to the general reader.

The Cascade Companions series addresses the challenge by publishing books that combine academic rigor with broad appeal and readability. They aim to introduce nonspecialist readers to that vital storehouse of authors, documents, themes, histories, arguments, and movements that comprise this heritage with brief yet compelling volumes.

RECENT TITLES IN THIS SERIES:

Feminism and Christianity by Caryn D. Griswold
Angels, Worms, and Bogeys by Michelle A. Clifton-Soderstrom
Christianity and Politics by C. C. Pecknold
A Way to Scholasticism by Peter S. Dillard
Theological Theodicy by Daniel Castelo
The Letter to the Hebrews in Social-Scientific Perspective
    by David A. deSilva
Basil of Caesarea by Andrew Radde-Galwitz
A Guide to St. Symeon the New Theologian by Hannah Hunt
Reading John by Christopher W. Skinner
Forgiveness by Anthony Bash
Jacob Arminius by Rustin Brian
The Rule of Faith: A Guide by Everett Ferguson
Jeremiah: Prophet Like Moses by Jack Lundbom
Richard Hooker: A Companion to His Life and Work by W. Bradford Littlejohn
Scripture's Knowing: A Companion to Biblical Epistemology by Dru Johnson
John Calvin by Donald McKim
Rudolf Bultmann: A Companion to His Theology by David Congdon
The U.S. Immigration Crisis: Toward an Ethics of Place
    by Miguel A. De La Torre
Theologia Crucis: A Companion to the Theology of the Cross
    by Robert Cady Saler
Theology and Science Fiction by James F. McGrath
Virtue: An Introduction to Theory and Practice by Olli-Pekka Vainio
Approaching Job by Andrew Zack Lewis
Reading Kierkegaard I: Fear and Trembling by Paul Martens
Deuteronomy: Law and Covenant by Jack R. Lundbom
The Becoming of God: Process Theology, Philosophy, and Multireligious Engagement by Roland Faber

A COMPANION TO THE BOOK OF REVELATION

DAVID L. MATHEWSON

CASCADE *Books* · Eugene, Oregon

A COMPANION TO THE BOOK OF REVELATION

Cascade Companions

Copyright © 2020 David L. Mathewson. All rights reserved. Except for brief quotations in critical publications or reviews, no part of this book may be reproduced in any manner without prior written permission from the publisher. Write: Permissions, Wipf and Stock Publishers, 199 W. 8th Ave., Suite 3, Eugene, OR 97401.

Cascade Books
An Imprint of Wipf and Stock Publishers
199 W. 8th Ave., Suite 3
Eugene, OR 97401

www.wipfandstock.com

PAPERBACK ISBN: 978-1-5326-7816-5
HARDCOVER ISBN: 978-1-5326-7817-2
EBOOK ISBN: 978-1-5326-7818-9

Cataloguing-in-Publication data:

Names: Mathewson, David L., author.

Title: A companion to the book of Revelation / by David L. Mathewson.

Description: Eugene, OR: Cascade Books, 2020 | Series: Cascade Companions | Includes bibliographical references and index.

Identifiers: ISBN 978-1-5326-7816-5 (paperback) | ISBN 978-1-5326-7817-2 (hardcover) | ISBN 978-1-5326-7818-9 (ebook)

Subjects: LCSH: Bible. N.T. Revelation—Criticism, interpretation, etc. | Bible. N.T. Revelation—Theology.

Classification: BS2825.52 M38 2020 (print) | BS2825.52 (ebook)

Manufactured in the U.S.A. 03/11/20

CONTENTS

Acknowledgments • vii

1. Reading the Book of Revelation • 1
2. Revelation: Story, Structure, and Symbols • 19
3. The Messages from the Risen Lord to Seven Churches (Revelation 1–3) • 38
4. A Vision of Heaven's Throne Room (Revelation 4–5) • 57
5. Visions of Judgment and Salvation I (Revelation 6–16) • 71
6. Visions of Judgment and Salvation II (Revelation 17–20) • 97
7. A Final Vision of Future Salvation: The New Creation (Revelation 21–22) • 116
8. The Relevance of Revelation for the Church Today • 134

Bibliography • 145
Scripture Index • 149

ACKNOWLEDGMENTS

I AM EXTREMELY GRATEFUL for the invitation to write this book. It represents my current reflections on the book of Revelation, which always seem to be in development. Furthermore, it has given me the opportunity to think through more carefully a number of sections of this book at a level I had not done before. In addition, it has forced me to write in a way that is more accessible to a wider Christian audience. Therefore, I am grateful to the churches in the Denver, CO area that have allowed me to "test" some of the material found in this book. I would be remiss if I did not express my debt of gratitude to the many fine commentators who have been my companions and reliable guides in writing this volume. The footnotes inadequately reflect the influence that the works of others have had on my thinking.

The writing of this book also gives me an opportunity to thank two of my professors while I was a student at Denver Seminary who are responsible for my interest in

Acknowledgments

the book of Revelation. Bill Klein assigned to me (initially against my will!) a paper on the Millennium in Revelation 20 for a class on New Testament theology. This paper first introduced me to the fascinating world of apocalyptic literature and interpreting Revelation. Later, Craig Blomberg encouraged me to write a paper for a course on New Testament criticism on interpreting Revelation 12–13 in light of its genre. Both of those projects sparked an interest in Revelation, and the fire has not died down. This book owes its existence to those two individuals.

1

READING THE BOOK OF REVELATION

INTRODUCTION

THE PURPOSE OF THIS companion is to be just that—a companion on your journey through the book of Revelation. It is meant to provide a short guide to reading through this unique biblical book, in order to enhance your reading experience. But before getting into the book of Revelation itself, the remainder of this chapter and the next chapter will briefly introduce you to a number of key issues that will help you get off on the right foot in your reading venture. One of the most important questions that we must ask is, What kind of book is Revelation? How we answer this question will determine what we expect to find in the last book of the Bible.

WHAT KIND OF BOOK IS REVELATION?

The book of Revelation claims to be written by an individual named John (1:1, 4, 9; 22:8), but does not further identify him, except to show that he writes as a prophet (1:3; 22:6, 10) and was presumably well-known by the churches in first-century Asia Minor. Clearly, John situates himself within the tradition of the Old Testament prophets of the past (e.g., Isaiah, Ezekiel).[1] Early church tradition assigns authorship of Revelation to the Apostle John, who was presumably also responsible for the Fourth Gospel and 1–3 John. Irenaeus (AD 130–202) concluded that Revelation was written near the end of the reign of Domitian by "John, the disciple of our Lord" (*Against Heresies*, iv.14.1; v.30.3). This view was followed by other early witnesses such as Justin Martyr, Clement of Alexandria, and Tertullian. But it was questioned early on by others (e.g., Eusebius of Caesarea, AD 260–340)[2] and continues to be questioned by many scholars today. However, the similarities with John's Gospel and the possibility that the differences in style can be accounted for by the unique literary genre and circumstances of Revelation could still allow for common authorship,[3] and early church tradition is strong in attributing it to John the apostle. It is impossible to be absolutely certain about the identity of the author, but John the apostle is as plausible as any proposal. John clearly claims to deliver an authoritative message revealed to him through Jesus Christ (1:1–3). The most commonly accepted date of Revelation is towards the end of the reign of the Roman Emperor Domitian (AD 81–96) in AD 95–96. Though not a lot depends on dating the book precisely,

1. Bauckham, *Theology of Revelation*, 5.
2. Eusebius, *Hist. Eccl.* 3.39.
3. Paul, *Revelation*, 7–11.

a date in the later part of the first century during the reign of Domitian remains likely.

What kind of book did John write? In a sense this chapter is foundational for the rest of this companion volume, since it establishes the interpretive framework for how we approach and read Revelation overall. Interpretation of any given piece of writing is governed partly by what kind of literature it is (the term for this is *genre*). Even today, we do not read a business letter (or email, more likely) in the same way that we read a novel, nor the cartoon section of the newspaper in the same way we read the front-page headlines. We expect different things from a science fiction movie and a CNN documentary. All of these are different kinds of *genres* and they create different reader expectations and communicate in different ways with different rules for understanding them. In the same way, the Bible consists of different types of literature, or *genres*, such as narrative (Genesis, Gospels, Acts), poetry (Psalms), prophecy (Isaiah, Jeremiah), or epistles (Paul's writings, 1 Peter, James).[4] All of them require a different set of principles for interpretation consistent with the kind of literature they are. Most scholars recognize that the book of Revelation actually consists of a combination of at least three different literary *genres* that would have been familiar to a first-century Christian audience and that are important for interpreting Revelation: an *Apocalypse*, a *Prophecy*, and a *Letter*.[5]

---

4. Klein et al., *Introduction to Biblical Interpretation*; Fee and Stuart, *How to Read the Bible*.

5. Bauckham, *Theology of Revelation*, 1–17; Mathewson, "Revelation in Recent Genre Criticism."

Apocalypse

When we hear the term "apocalypse" we frequently think of end of the world, mass destruction, World War III, worldwide pandemic, and the decimation of civilization, conceptions perpetrated by the entertainment industry. But the term apocalypse as used with reference to the book of Revelation refers to something very different. More accurately, biblical scholars today use the term to refer to a type of literature that would have been prevalent during the period of time of roughly 200 BC to AD 200. The term "Revelation" itself comes from the Greek word *apokalypsis* found in Revelation 1:1 ("a *revelation* of Jesus Christ"), from which we get the word "apocalypse," meaning literally *an unveiling or uncovering*. The word apocalypse then came to be used in our modern day of a specific kind of ancient literature that resembled the book of Revelation and that was common around the time of the first century when John saw and recorded his vision. Besides Revelation, the only other biblical examples of an apocalypse are the book of Daniel, and parts of Ezekiel and Zechariah. But there are numerous examples of this kind of literature outside of the Old and New Testaments, books such as 1 Enoch, 2 Baruch, 4 Ezra, the Shepherd of Hermas, and several others. Translations of these works can be found collected in books,[6] or even online. But what was an apocalypse? An apocalypse was a narrative account of someone's visionary experience. It recorded or narrated what it was the author saw in a dream or vision. Furthermore, the vision was communicated in highly metaphorical language. An apocalypse would refer to actual persons, places, and events, in the seer's day and in the future, but it communicated these in highly symbolic, rather than

6. Charlesworth, *Old Testament Pseudepigrapha*.

literal, language. It was meant to address a crisis or other issue that the seer and his audience of that day were facing. This type of literature was meant to console and to exhort people to appropriate action in this situation of crisis (e.g., oppression by a foreign empire).

An apocalypse "unveiled" or "uncovered" the true nature of things through a vision that offered an alternative perspective on the world so that the readers could see their situation in a new light and respond in an appropriate manner. It was not meant to confuse them, or hide something from them. It was meant to unveil and communicate the truth. An apocalypse provided a divine, heavenly perspective on what was going on in the world, a perspective that challenged the dominant cultural perspectives of how the world should be viewed. Apocalypses show that the world is not really as it appears. They uncover the truth about the world and the situation of the audience: God is in control, not the dominant empires of the day. Symbolism was the predominant mode of communication in apocalyptic works. The symbolism was meant to evoke a response in the readers in a way that more straightforward speech could not. Therefore, when John tells us that he saw a seven-headed beast in his vision in Revelation 13, he is most likely referring to the Roman Empire. But what is the effect of describing Rome in this way? John could have just said to his readers, "Watch out for Rome. It is an evil, violent, godless empire that means you harm. It is not all that it is cracked up to be." But it is more effective, and evocative, to say, "I saw a beast coming up out of the sea, having ten horns and seven heads" (13:1). The seven-headed beast would have evoked notions of chaos, evil, oppression, and terror in the first readers, exactly how John wants his readers to view Rome. Seen in this light, the readers should be less than enthusiastic about associating with the great city and enjoying all it had to offer them.

Since it was a fairly common type of literature around the time of the first century (we have no close literary analogies to this type of literature today), the audience of Revelation would have been familiar with what they were hearing/reading when confronted with John's book. In other words, an apocalypse was intended to help its first audience make sense of their world and whatever crisis or problem they were facing. Revelation tells the story of the first-century churches of Asia Minor, but a story that is couched in metaphors in an apocalyptic vision.

Prophecy

Revelation is also a *Prophecy*. However, biblical prophecy is very different than most modern-day conceptions of prophecy. Most modern-day readers think of prophecy as "prediction of the future," usually the distant future. It is as if the prophet gazed into a crystal ball and saw distant times, places, and events centuries down the road from his own day. But predicting the future was not the main focus of biblical prophecy. Scholars often distinguish between two functions of biblical prophecy: *foretelling* and *forthtelling*.[7] Usually we think of prophecy primarily in terms of *foretelling*, that is, predicting the future in advance. While prophecy does contain future predictions, biblical prophecy is far more interested in *forthtelling*, that is, proclaiming a message to the present time of the first readers, a message of comfort, exhortation, or warning. John calls his book a prophecy several times (1:3; 22:7, 10, 18–19) and he consistently alludes to Old Testament prophetic

---

7. Klein et al., *Introduction to Biblical Interpretation*, 462.

texts. Once more, the first readers would have understood what it meant for John to call his work a prophecy, that John was primarily *forthtelling*, communicating a message of comfort and prophetic warning to his churches. In fact, the seven "letters" to the seven churches in Revelation 2–3 are more accurately understood as prophetic messages that comfort but mostly exhort and warn the churches. Revelation is addressing the first-century churches' situations and needs, as biblical prophecy does. John clearly stands in the line of the Old Testament prophets like Isaiah and Ezekiel. Like them, John's primary concern is not prediction of the future (though there are visions of the future in Revelation), but exhortation and comfort for God's people who are under oppression or straying from the covenant that God made with them.

Perhaps most importantly, like the Old Testament prophets of the past (Isaiah, Jeremiah, Ezekiel, Joel, etc.), John offers a stinging critique of the dominant empire of the day: Rome. In the past it was empires such as Egypt, Tyre, Assyria, and Babylon that were the subjects of prophetic critique. They were exposed for their godlessness, violence, oppression, exploitation, and illegitimate use of power. Now John, as a prophet in line with his Old Testament predecessors, picks up their language in order to level the same critique against the Roman Empire of the day, once again to dissuade his Christian audience from associating too closely with Rome and becoming entangled in its idolatrous system. As a prophecy, Revelation exposes Rome for what it really is and communicates a warning to seven churches that are feeling the pressure to compromise with the first-century pagan Roman Empire. At the same time, John predicts the demise of all such empires when Christ returns to set up his kingdom.

Letter

Finally, Revelation is also a *Letter*. It is easy to miss this in the midst of the blizzard of fantastic images that dominate Revelation. Revelation begins and ends just like a typical first-century letter, such as one of Paul's letters (e.g., Romans, Galatians, Ephesians). It contains a letter greeting (1:4–5) and a letter closing (22:21). What is the significance of this literary feature? First-century letters were what are known as *occasional*, that is, they were written in response to specific circumstances and situations of specific readers. Letters in the first century would have communicated information that addressed the needs of the first readers to whom they were written. This means that letters would have communicated information that was accessible and understandable to the first audience. Therefore, as a letter Revelation is communicating information that meets the needs and addresses the circumstances of the seven churches situated in ancient Asia Minor (Rev 2–3). Consequently, it must have been understood by the first readers, not a message hidden for a later century or generation of readers to finally discover, a message about which the first readers were completely in the dark. As a letter, the book of Revelation is a pastoral response to the crisis that the Christians in Asia Minor faced living in the midst of the Roman Empire of the first century.

In summary, Revelation consists of three literary genres that would have been fairly common in the first-century world and with which the readers would have been familiar. When they heard Revelation read (1:3),[8]

---

8. Rev 1:3 pronounces a blessing on the one who reads (singular) and those who hear (plural) the book. This is how Revelation would have been first received by the first readers in the seven churches in Asia Minor: someone would have read the book in its entirety to them.

they would have known what it was they were listening to. Furthermore, all three genres would have communicated information that was comprehensible to the original readers. The readers would have expected Revelation was going to communicate something that would shed light on their unique issues and problems, albeit in the form of a vision and communicated through metaphors. Revelation is a book about the first-century Christians and their world, not about our twenty-first-century world, though as God's word it is still relevant to us today.

THE HISTORICAL CONTEXT OF REVELATION

So what is the specific crisis or problem that the book of Revelation addresses that we must recover in order to understand the book more accurately? As we have already hinted at, the historical setting for Revelation can be found in the messages to the seven churches in chapters 2–3. Rather than just a tertiary section, these seven messages are crucial to understanding the entire book of Revelation, for they provide the historical backdrop and setting that occasioned the vision and its subsequent recording in this unique book.[9] If the book of Revelation was meant to respond to and shed light on the readers' own situation, we need to understand something about that situation.

A common (mis)perception of the book is that it was written to persecuted Christians under Roman rule (probably Domitian). Suffering and persecution are indeed dominant themes throughout the book. However, there is debate as to the extent to which significant persecution did or did not take place in the first-century Roman Empire

---

9. Culy, *Book of Revelation*.

during this time.[10] Furthermore, there is little evidence that Domitian, if Revelation was written at the end of the first century, leveled any official persecution against Christians. If anything, any pressure or persecution would have likely come at the local level, by officials who were keen to foster and maintain allegiance to Rome. A more significant problem appears to be willingness by Christians to compromise with the Roman system. The seven cities to which John addresses his apocalyptic, prophetic letter were all firmly ensconced in the Roman imperial world. When Revelation was written, Rome was the dominant empire of the day, and its influence spread far and wide. Moreover, Rome assumed and told a narrative about itself: Rome was the "Eternal City" (*Roma Aeterna*) chosen and favored by the gods. It brought peace (*Pax Romana*) to the entire world, along with stability and order.[11] Rome was believed to be the center of the world. Besides a number of pagan and religious influences, one of the biggest threats to Christians in those seven cities was emperor worship, a system of demonstrating allegiance to the emperor, which reinforced this narrative about the divine selection and power of the Roman Empire. All of the cities had imperial temples, shrines, altars, and other visible reminders of the imperial power. Even the coinage of ancient Rome reminded inhabitants of and reinforced this story of Roman power. Local authorities were keen to enforce loyalty to Rome through emperor worship, since Rome brought peace, salvation, and prosperity. In cities like Thyatira, trade guilds would have required expressions of gratitude and loyalty to Rome. To refuse to participate in veneration

---

10. For a detailed discussion that disputes the view that Revelation was written in response to a crisis involving persecution under the Roman Empire, see Thompson, *The Book of Revelation*.

11. deSilva, *Unholy Allegiances*, 21–34.

to the emperor would be to fail to show the appropriate loyalty and gratitude to Rome.[12]

The options for Christians living in such a situation were clear. First, one could see loyalty to Rome and worship of the emperor as inconsistent with worship of the true God and his Christ, and refuse to participate. The result was suffering in the form of persecution, ostracism, and perhaps other forms of oppression, especially economic. So far John only mentions one person who has actually been put to death, a man named Antipas in the city of Pergamum (3:13), though John thinks there are more on the horizon (6:9–11; 13:9–10). However, only two churches that John addresses receive a positive evaluation for taking a stand and suffering for it—the churches of Smyrna (2:8–11) and Philadelphia (3:7–13). Second, the opposite response would be to compromise with Rome and even become complacent with one's situation under the Roman Empire, perhaps thinking allegiance to Rome was simply their civic duty. Five of the churches receive a negative evaluation because they have become complacent or have compromised with Rome to some degree, some getting wealthy off the Roman unjust economic system (Laodicea in 3:14–22).

It is to this situation or crisis that John responds by recording a vision given by God. John offers a prophetic critique of the Roman Empire, exposing its ungodliness, violence, oppression, and illegitimate use of power. John provides a counter set of images and symbols to those offered by Rome's imperial system and culture. Revelation is meant to show that things are not as they appear, the dominant cultural version of Rome's story is not the correct one, and Rome is not all that it appears to be. God is

12. deSilva, *Unholy Allegiances*, 30.

on his throne and in control of history and of the world, and God and the Lamb stand at the center of the universe and alone are worthy of worship and allegiance. Only God and the Lamb can bring true peace and salvation. John calls on Christians to overcome and resist the temptation to compromise by giving allegiance to Rome and its evil system. To those churches suffering persecution at the hands of the empire, the vision of Revelation is a message of comfort. But to those churches who are complacent and compromising, John's vision would function as a message of warning to repent and cease compromising. Christians must follow God and the Lamb, no matter what the consequences. The entire book of Revelation must be understood in light of this historical context to which it is a response.

It is important to note, then, that Revelation 4–22, the "vision proper" of Revelation, is not some section unrelated to chapters 2–3, or a record of events that take place centuries after the events in the seven messages to the churches. Rather, chapters 4–22 refer to the same events and situations referred to in the seven letters in 2–3. If chapters 2–3 are more direct prophetic evaluations of the churches, then 4–22 will say the same thing and cover the exact same ground as 2–3, but now in the form of an apocalyptic vision. Chapters 4–22 are the story of the first-century church in 2–3 in the form of symbols and metaphors. In other words, each of the seven churches would have read Revelation differently, depending on their circumstances.[13]

---

13. Culy, *Book of Revelation*.

THE BEGINNING AND END OF REVELATION

There are further clues at the very beginning of Revelation and at its very conclusion for how John expected his book to be understood. And these clues make it very clear that John thought he was communicating to his readers information that they would be able to grasp and understand. In other words, he expected them to make sense of his book, since he was addressing the specific situations of the seven churches in Asia Minor.

First, at the very beginning of his book John pronounces a blessing on the one who hears the words of his book and who takes them to heart or keeps them (1:3). To "keep" the words of Revelation meant to obey them. The entire book of Revelation is a book meant to be obeyed, not to be used for constructing end-time charts or speculating how close any given generation is to the end. If Revelation is only comprehensible to a twenty-first-century audience, and if the first readers in Asia Minor were in the dark about the meaning of Revelation, then the call for the original first-century readers to obey the book in 1:3 would be extremely frustrating, if not downright deceptive. The fact that John expects his first readers (not just us) to obey his book assumes that they could understand what it was about. This is consistent with the fact that John writes in three literary types that his readers in the first century would have been familiar with—Apocalypse, Prophecy, and Letter (see above).

Second, at the very end of the book an angel is giving John final instructions about the vision he saw and recorded in the entire book of Revelation. In the end the angel tells John not to seal up the words of the prophecy of this scroll (22:10). This is the exact opposite of what Daniel was told to do in his vision in Daniel 12:4; there he was told to seal his book up until the time of the end. To seal up a book meant to keep its contents hidden until a future time, the time when they would be fulfilled. But in Revelation 22:10 John is told just the opposite: he is not to seal up his book, because the time is near. The fact that the time was at hand or near meant that the events of Revelation were about to be or were already being fulfilled in John's day through the person of Jesus Christ. This was a book for his first readers, not for some future time or generation, and therefore, John is instructed not to seal it up. It communicated a message for the first readers, who are living in the time of fulfillment, where Christ's life, death, and resurrection have already inaugurated the end times (see Matt 12:28; 1 Cor 10:11; Heb 1:2). Therefore, Revelation begins and ends with statements that make it clear that the visions and their images were to be understood within the context of the first audience and their historical situation, not hidden for some later generation to figure out. Furthermore, it is a book meant to be obeyed by its readers.

INTERPRETING THE BOOK OF REVELATION

So how should all of this make a difference in how we interpret Revelation? What interpretive strategies should guide us as we read it? The following six reading strategies, or principles of interpretation, grow out of the kind of book that Revelation is.

1. *Revelation was a book meant to be understood by its first readers.* John's book, as strange as it may seem to the modern reader, would have made sense to his first readers and helped them come to grips with the temptations, fears, and threats they faced as Christians living in the Roman Empire. Therefore, we must

start by asking what the first-century Christians in Ephesus, or Pergamum, or Smyrna, or Thyatira, or Laodicea would have understood by it, and what John would likely have intended to communicate to them. Any interpretation that John could never have intended and his first readers could never have understood is probably incorrect.

2. *This means that Revelation must be interpreted in light of its historical context.* Related to the first reading strategy, perhaps with more than any other book in the New Testament, we need to grasp the historical context that occasioned Revelation. It was written to seven historical churches living in a specific time and historical situation. Their unique cultural and historical circumstances living under the shadow of the Roman Empire and facing such threats as emperor worship, pressure to compromise, and persecution must be kept firmly in mind when interpreting the book, so as not to read our own ideas and background back into the text.

3. *Revelation communicates in metaphors, not literally.* While Revelation refers to real persons, places, and events, it does not describe them literally. The primary mode of communication in Revelation is symbolism or metaphor (see next chapter). This means that due to the kind of literature it is, Revelation is not to be interpreted literally. John *sees* a seven-headed beast in his vision, but the beast *refers* to the Roman Empire. Often the most difficult task of the interpreter is to discern what person, events, or places in John's day, or in the future, are the ones that Revelation is referring to. Symbols had evocative power, engaging the emotions and imagination, as well as the intellect.

John's symbols come out of his and his readers' background and would have been familiar to the churches to which he first wrote.

4. *John draws on images primarily from the Old Testament but also the Greco-Roman world to describe his vision.* One of the keys to understand the meaning of John's symbols is to understand their source (see next chapter). Revelation is replete with symbols that draw on the Old Testament. Nearly every verse contains an allusion to an Old Testament text, so it is almost impossible to understand John's vision without knowledge of the Old Testament. Often, John's allusions carry with them the broader context of the Old Testament texts.[14] But some of John's symbols were also at home in the Greco-Roman world (e.g., a dragon-type figure that pursues a woman about to give birth in Revelation 12 reflected a common myth in the Greco-Roman world).

5. *Revelation is a mixture of references to the present and to the future.* Revelation does contain visions of the distant future, that is, the second coming of Christ and the wrap-up of human history (Rev 19–22). However, Revelation more commonly refers to the present time or near future of the first-century audience, Christians living in the cities within the Roman Empire in Asia Minor, helping them to make sense of what is going on. It would not make sense if Revelation simply told them how history would end some day off in the distant future. Rather, Revelation is meant to shed light on their present circumstances. Even when John offers visions of the end of the world, it is to motivate God's people to live life

14. Mathewson, *New Heaven and a New Earth*.

responsibly in the present, to provide hope and staying power to the end.

6. *Revelation is intended to inspire godly living and obedience.* The main goal of Revelation is to transform the lives of its hearers/readers, not to predict a future sequence of events. Its main function is pastoral and hortatory. Revelation's visions are meant to provide a divine perspective on the world so that the audience will respond appropriately. It is intended to get Christians to follow and obey God and the Lamb in true discipleship, no matter what the consequences. It is a call for God's people to maintain their faithful witness to Jesus Christ and the Gospel to the very end. Revelation is a prophetic warning and encouragement for Christians to obey its message. Any interpretation of Revelation that does not start with this is off on the wrong foot. Revelation calls for perseverance in discipleship and godly living, worked out in the midst of pagan Imperial Roman rule.

THE CENTRAL QUESTION OF THE BOOK

At the heart of Revelation's message is the question: Who is in control of all things? Who is worthy of allegiance? The Roman Empire answered this question in the form of emperor worship and displays of power and allegiance to Rome. But Revelation provides a counterclaim by demonstrating that only God and the Lamb are worthy of worship and allegiance. God and the Lamb and their throne, not Rome and its emperors, are at the center of the cosmos (see Rev 4–5). To worship any other entity is nothing less than idolatry. Revelation presents an image of God seated on the throne, in sovereign control of all things, the One who created all things, and who has acted to redeem humanity and creation. Revelation's visions orient God's people to who is at the center of reality: Who is really the Lord of the universe? Who is really in control? And therefore, who is really worthy of allegiance, adoration, and worship?[15] In the face of claims to the contrary, John's book is deeply doxological and functions to inspire unqualified and absolute allegiance to God and the Lamb, no matter what the consequences it might bring for those living within the reaches of the pagan Roman Empire.

REFLECTION

1. How does your understanding of Revelation as an Apocalypse challenge the way you may have previously read the book of Revelation?

2. Revelation was addressed to seven churches, five of which were compromising with the pagan empire of the day. What implications does this have for how you see Revelation addressing the church today?

---

15. Bauckham, *Theology of Revelation*, 9.

2

REVELATION: STORY, STRUCTURE, AND SYMBOLS

THE STORY OF REVELATION

THE BOOK OF REVELATION provides a fitting climax to the entire canon of Scripture. As such it concludes the story of God's redemptive plan for all creation and humanity begun in Genesis 1–2. It gathers up the hopes and images from the Old Testament prophetic texts and reasserts their fulfillment in light of the story of Christ's death and resurrection. Revelation also contains a story within itself. John's unique book claims to be a written narrative of a vision that he had. As a narrative Revelation tells a story, though it is a very different story from what we have seen before in the New Testament (Gospels, Acts). It is a story told with fantastic images and metaphors. As a story, it has characters and a story line, or plot, tension, and resolution. The following is only a summary of the main characters and the story line of John's Revelation.

The Main Characters

All stories feature characters that move the plot forward, usually consisting of protagonists and antagonists. There are a number of key characters that play important roles in Revelation's visionary world. The following is just a summary of the main protagonists and their role in John's story:

> *God, the one seated on the throne*: God is the originator of the vision (1:1) but is arguably the main character throughout the entire book. His titles (e.g., Lord God Almighty; the One who was and is and is to come; the first and last) and his throne indicate his sovereign and eternal rule over all things and over the story of Revelation. He is the creator of all that exists, and it is God's intention to establish his rule throughout all creation.
>
> *Jesus Christ:* Jesus Christ is God's agent for establishing his kingdom on earth and for implementing God's plan for redemption. The person of Christ appears in different forms throughout Revelation. Jesus first appears as the Son of Man, a majestic exalted figure who addresses his seven churches and who will come to judge. He also shares in the very identity of God, as the one who is the "alpha and omega," the "first and last." He is the king of kings and ruler of the kings of the earth. The main way that Jesus is portrayed in Revelation is as a Lamb (5:6). The primary feature of the Lamb is that he suffered and is slain and therefore redeems a

people for God from the earth. Yet he too shares in the sovereign rule of God, sharing his throne. It is through the Lamb that God's will is to be accomplished on earth in redeeming a people. Jesus is also portrayed as a rider on a white horse who will return as a judge over all the earth (19:11–21).

The Spirit: The Spirit does not play the overt, visible role that God and the Lamb play, but is present nonetheless. The Spirt is present before the throne in the form of seven spirits (4:5) and is sent out into all the earth (5:6). The Spirit inspires John in his visionary experience (1:10; 4:2; 17:3; 21:10). The Spirit also gives life to God's people in the new creation (21:6; 22:1).

Angels: Angels play a key role in representing the people of God, and indeed all creation, in heaven in their worship of God and the Lamb (Rev 4–5). They are also instrumental in carrying out the judgment plagues poured out on the earth, and they guide John in his visionary experience. They are even responsible for defeating the primary antagonist, the dragon. Their voice is often heard interpreting the significance of certain events.

The people of God, the church: The church consists of those people that the Lamb has redeemed from the earth. They are also to be God's faithful witnesses on earth to the reality of God and his kingdom and to witness to the nations, especially in the face of suffering. Therefore, they are called to faithfulness and warned of the danger of compromising with the evil world system. There are a number of metaphors used to depict the church in its various roles: the 144,000 warriors (7:1–8); the two witnesses (11:3–12); the offspring of the woman (12:13–17); the New Jerusalem, the consummated bride of the Lamb (21:2, 9–21).

However, stories also have their antagonists. The primary antagonists in the drama of the book of Revelation, who oppose God and the Lamb, his people, and the establishment of God's kingdom on earth are the following:

The dragon, Satan: The dragon is the primary antagonist to God and his sovereign rule. The present earth is his kingdom. He is also the primary source behind the persecution against the church (esp. Rev 12).

The two beasts: The two beastly figures are cohorts of the dragon, and carry out his will on earth in the form of persecution of the people of God and directing worship and allegiance towards the dragon. Along with the dragon, the two beasts fill out the "unholy trinity" that stands in sharp contrast and opposition to the Trinity of protagonists, God, Christ the Lamb, and the Holy Spirit (Rev 12–13).

Babylon: Babylon is the great city that embodies all that is opposed to God and his purposes (Rev 17–18). It offers wealth and prosperity, exploits the nations, is the place where the saints suffer, and stands in opposition to the New Jerusalem/bride in 21:1—22:5.

Those who dwell on the earth: These are those people who have clearly sided with the dragon and the two beasts and they harm God's people.

There also appear to be a couple of characters that play more of a neutral role in Revelation's story, for the most part. They are under the rule of the dragon and the beasts, but are the object of God's concern and redemptive activity. In a sense, they are caught between the protagonists and antagonists.[1]

> *The nations*: They are tempted to and often give allegiance to the dragon and beasts, yet they are the objects of God's redemptive activity and the church's faithful witnesses who are "from every tribe language people and nation." On the one hand they are hostile towards the people of God and subject to judgment (11:7–10; 19:19–21), but on the other hand they end up in the New Jerusalem (21:24–26; 22:2).

> *The earth itself*: The earth can also be considered a character in the story. The earth is under the dominion of the dragon, and the place of his persecuting activity and the inhabitants that give allegiance to the dragon. Yet it is also the place of the church's witnessing activity, and God's ultimate intention is to reclaim and redeem it also and fill it with his glorious presence (21:1—22:5).

John's Story

There are probably different ways to tell the story of Revelation;[2] the following is one way of envisioning the plot. The first three chapters of Revelation begin by introducing the main protagonists—God, Jesus Christ, the Spirit, and the churches, the people of God that he has redeemed from all the nations of the earth. Jesus is the

---

1. See especially Morales, *Christ, Shepherd of the Nations*.

2. Barr, *Tales of the End*; Gorman, *Reading Revelation Responsibly*, 116–37.

exalted Son of Man who has already defeated death and is the Lord of the cosmos. The church is to be God's faithful witnesses throughout the earth, to represent his kingdom and presence in the world, and not give in to the pressure to conform to the world. The drama then switches to a heavenly scene in Revelation 4–5, where God and the Lamb are seated on the throne in heaven, and the Spirit, the one who is sent into all the earth to accomplish God's will, is before the throne. As much as Revelation may be a story about the situation of the churches in first-century Asia Minor, it projects this story on a cosmic screen, revealing a larger conflict between God and the evil forces of the cosmos.[3] The way God's will is going to be accomplished is through the slain Lamb, who shares the throne with God. Heaven is portrayed as a place of order, where God's sovereignty and will are completely acknowledged and realized. All heaven worships God and the Lamb on the throne. The question that this phase of the story raises is, How is the scene in heaven ultimately going to be accomplished on earth? How will God's sovereignty that is acknowledged in heaven come to be realized throughout all creation, where it is presently contested and rejected by the dragon, Satan, and the empires of the world that he inspires? How will God reclaim all creation and people from every nation, people, tribe, language to be his people? The rest of Revelation's story will answer this question. The scene then switches to earth in chapter 6, as the scene in heaven in chapters 4–5 begins to be worked out on earth in the rest of the book. God's will and plan for all the earth to come under his sovereign reign is to be accomplished through the work of the slain Lamb. The role of the church is to maintain their faithful witness to this reality, even in the

---

3. Barr, *Tales of the End*, 2.

face of suffering and death. The reality to which the people of God, the church, witness is that God is the sovereign ruler who has redeemed people through the Lamb to be his "kingdom of priests." God is already unleashing his judgments on this present world in the form of seals, trumpets, and bowl plagues, with the intention that humanity will repent. The execution of these judgments is aided by the angels. Ultimately God will judge the great city, Babylon (chs. 17–18) and all that opposes his will and intention to redeem all creation and bring salvation to all people (chs. 19–20) to make room for a just world (21:1–22:5).

In contrast to heaven, earth is a place of chaos, under the dominion of the dragon, Satan. The chaos is heightened by demonic figures consisting of a chaotic combination of animal-like features (9:1–11). The primary conflict is that God's will and the faithful witness of his people to the sacrificial death of the Lamb for all people are opposed by the dragon, the primary antagonist, and his two cohorts, the two beastly figures, whose job it is to deceive the nations that God wants to redeem and to persecute the church whose faithful witness to the reality of God (his judgments and salvation) and Christ they are trying to extinguish. The heart of the conflict is found in Revelation 12–13. In this story within the larger story, a dragon pursues a woman who is about to give birth. Frustrated at his inability to destroy the child, he goes after the woman and eventually her offspring (ch. 12). He is aided in his warfare against the woman and her offspring by two beastly figures (ch. 13). However, the dragon, Satan, and therefore also his two beastly cohorts, have already been dealt a blow through the death of Jesus Christ and his faithful witnesses, though the dragon's persecuting activity continues. The earth is a place under the dominion of the dragon, even though his reign is limited.

Through the faithful witness of his people, and through the judgment and removal of all that opposes his will, especially the dragon and two beasts (Rev 19–20), a will that is perfectly realized in heaven but presently contested on earth, God brings salvation to his people, reclaims the nations, and ultimately redeems the entire earth (21:1—22:5). The New Jerusalem has replaced Babylon, and the creation under the old order wrecked by sin and death and under the dominion of the dragon and the beasts is now renewed and replaced with a new creation. All that thwarts the realization of God's justice and sovereignty has been removed in a series of judgments (chs. 6–20), people from every tribe, tongue, people, and language have been redeemed, and the heavenly scene from Revelation 4–5 has now become a reality on earth (chs. 21–22). The heavenly dwelling place of God has now become one with the earth, and God and the Lamb's throne is now in the center of the new creation. The nations, who were previously deceived by and under the rule of the dragon, have been redeemed and stream into the city, and all God's people now serve Him. All of this is framed within a visionary experience that John has which he now communicates in the form of a letter to seven historical churches in Asia Minor.

As Richard Bauckham helpfully explains, Revelation 4–22 could be seen as an expansion of the Lord's Prayer (Matt 6:9–11): "Hallowed be your name, your kingdom come, your will be done, on earth as it is in heaven."[4] In Revelation 4–5 we see the part of the Lord's prayer that confesses that God's will is done in heaven. In these two chapters of Revelation, all heaven acknowledges God's

---

4. Bauckham, *Theology of Revelation*, 40.

sovereignty and will. The rest of the book of Revelation (chs. 6–22) is the story of how God's kingdom and will, acknowledged in heaven (chs. 4–5), become a reality on earth (chs. 21–22): "*on earth* as it is in heaven." Revelation 6–20 is the story of how that happens. In this sense the plot is sort of U-shaped. It begins with God's will perfectly realized in heaven (chs. 4–5). But earth is a place where God's will and kingdom are contested and contradicted and God's people who witness to it are persecuted. Through a series of judgments, and through the faithful witness of his people (chs. 6–20), the story ends with the scene in heaven from chapters 4–5 becoming a reality on earth, in a new creation where God's and the Lamb's will and kingdom are perfectly realized (chs. 21–22). It is within this larger story, of God's intention to reclaim the nations, all the kingdoms of the earth, and all creation for himself, that Revelation calls upon its audience to situate their own local stories in the cities of Asia Minor.

One other important observation to make about Revelation's story is the cyclical manner in which it moves forward. While the plot laid out above shows the unified story of Revelation, the book is not recording a temporally sequential series of events. The discerning reader will note that the way the book unfolds at times is more cyclical. That is, the author's visions cover the same time period, over and over, from different perspectives. So in the first sequence of seals in Revelation 6 the vision ends with a reference to the Great Day of the Lamb's wrath (vv. 15–17), an apparent reference to the coming of Christ at the very end of history. Yet we still have sixteen chapters left to go. Revelation 7 gives a glimpse of the people of God who have gone through the period of tribulation and now stand victorious before God's throne, yet once again the book is not finished. The end of the trumpet sequence in 11:15–19 also brings the reader to the final judgment and end of the world. But the narrative continues. Revelation 14 provides alternating visions of end-time salvation (vv. 14–16) and judgment (vv. 17–20). Then chapter 16 narrates once more the final judgments of God on humanity. Then we come to the end once more with more elaborate visions of final judgments (chs. 19–20) and salvation (chs. 21–22). The point is that while John's narrative is a unified story, it does not develop in a linear fashion but cycles through visions that cover the same ground—the period of the church's existence until the end-time judgment and salvation—from different perspectives and with different images. Therefore, it would be incorrect to think that John is giving the reader a precise timeline for how events in history and the end times will unfold.

STRUCTURAL FEATURES IN REVELATION

When exploring John's written record of his vision, what often gets overlooked in the midst of the fantastic visual images is that Revelation is an intricately designed literary work. It is not a mere patchwork of visions and indiscriminate symbols, but reveals a literary artist who has penned and structured his work with great care. There has been much debate as to how exactly to divide and outline the book of Revelation, with numerous proposals put forth for its structure, some of them quite elaborate. While this can be helpful, I will not provide another outline of the book, but instead highlight some of the structural features that provide guidance for navigating our way through Revelation and that provide structure and coherence to the book of Revelation. Here are some of the things to look for as you read through the book of Revelation.

Revelation: Story, Structure, and Symbols

"In the Spirit"

One of the key structural markers in the book of Revelation is the repeated phrase "in the Spirit."[5] It occurs four times, in 1:10; 4:2; 17:3; and 21:10, punctuating major visionary segments of John's Apocalypse. This suggests that at a macro level Revelation may be divided into four major sections: 1:10 introduces the inaugural vision of Jesus Christ, who will address the seven churches in chapters 2–3. Then 4:2 introduces the main visionary segment of the book, which begins with John's ascent to heaven (chs. 4–5). The two uses in 17:3 and 21:10 introduce the two climactic and contrasting visions of the entire book: the prostitute/Babylon (17:1—19:10) and the bride/New Jerusalem (21:1—22:5).

The Number "Seven"

One of the more important features of Revelation that provides unity and coherence is the use of the number seven as a structuring device. This number, which symbolizes perfection or completeness (see below), occurs as an organizing or unifying device in a number of places. The book is addressed to seven churches (1:11), and so there are seven prophetic messages to these churches (2–3). There are seven seals (6:1–17; 8:1), trumpets (8:6—9:21; 11:15–19), and bowls (16) that are unleashed by seven angels in the form of judgment plagues upon the cosmos. There is also a series of seven unnumbered visions toward the end of the book (chs. 19–21).

---

5. Bauckham, *Theology of Revelation*, 116.

A COMPANION TO THE BOOK OF REVELATION

Major Characters

The main characters—the one seated on the throne, the Lamb, the twenty-four elders, the angels with seven bowls, the dragon, the two beasts, the nations, the voice from the throne—appear throughout the book in various scenes and lend coherence to the text (see above).

Repeated Phrases and Names

Some form of the fourfold phrase "from every tribe, tongue people, and nation" occurs exactly seven times throughout the book (5:10; 7:9; 10:11; 11:9; 13:7; 14:6; 17:15). There are also seven beatitudes ("Blessed . . .") scattered throughout Revelation (1:3; 14:13; 16:15; 19:9; 20:6; 22:7, 14). Titles for God and the Lamb also occur in numerically significant ways throughout Revelation and similarly serve to link its visionary segments together. Some form of the title "the One who was and is and is to come" occurs five times (1:4, 8; 4:8; 11:17; 16:8), and a form of the "the alpha and omega, first and the last, beginning and the end" occurs four times, twice with reference to God (1:8; 21:6), and twice with reference to the Lamb (1:17; 22:13). The "Lord God Almighty" occurs seven times throughout the book (1:8; 4:8; 11:17; 15:3; 16:7; 19:6; 21:22).

Chapters 2–3 and the Rest of the Book

There are also clear links between the messages to the seven churches in Revelation 2–3 and the rest of the book, particularly the vision of chapter 1 and the final chapters (19–22). Most of the references to Jesus in the beginning of each of the messages in chapters 2–3 point back to a feature of Jesus' description in 1:12–16. Moreover, the promises to the one who overcomes at the end of each message correspond to elements later on in the New Jerusalem vision of 21:1—22:5. So for example, in the first message to the church in Ephesus the one who overcomes is promised a share in the tree of life in Paradise (2:7), which refers ahead to the tree of life in 22:2. In this way, Revelation 2–3 links backwards and forwards, tying the entire book together.[6]

There are other links throughout the work, but these should be sufficient to show that Revelation is a carefully constructed and structured work, with major patterns and clear linkages throughout the work. Though a number of outlines of Revelation might be plausible and shed light on different features of Revelation, it is more important to recognize that Revelation is more like a spider web, with links and inner connections backwards and forwards with numerical patterns and repeated phrases and images.

INTERPRETING REVELATION'S SYMBOLS

Probably the most distinctive feature of Revelation is its pervasive symbolism, which constitutes a challenge for the most serious reader. It is important to recognize that Revelation refers to real persons, places, and events, but describes them not literally but with symbols, or metaphors. John records what he sees in his vision, and the language that he uses corresponds closely to what he saw ("it was like . . .").

John's symbolism gets interpreted in two places in Revelation, providing an example of how John's language "works." In the first chapter John sees a vision of a Son of Man dressed in glorious splendor, holding seven

---

6. Paul, *Revelation*, 43–44.

lampstands and seven stars in 1:12–16. Jesus himself interprets the symbolism as follows in v. 20:

> Seven stars = the angels of the seven churches
>
> Seven lampstands = seven churches (in Asia Minor)

Thus, John sees seven stars and seven lampstands in his vision, but they are metaphors for something else; they refer to the seven angels of the churches and the seven churches that Jesus will address in chapters 2–3. The only other place where part of John's vision is interpreted for John, and for the readers, is in chapter 17. Here, John has a vision of a prostitute sitting on many waters, and riding a beast with seven heads and ten horns. The angel that accompanies John in his vision interprets the heads, and other features of the scene, for John. The seven heads actually get a dual interpretation; they are the seven hills upon which Babylon (historical Rome) sits, and they are seven kings (emperors) who rule; the ten horns are ten kings who receive a kingdom; the waters are the many people over which Babylon rules. These provide the pattern for interpreting the symbols in the rest of the book. John refers to real places, persons, and events, but he describes them metaphorically, not literally. This is much like a modern-day political cartoon, which refers to real persons and events in our modern-day political landscape, but it refers to them with highly symbolic language. One of the reasons for using symbolic language is that it is evocative and emotive, meant to bring about a powerful response in a way that more straightforward language cannot.

One of the keys to understanding John's language is to understand the source of his imagery from the world of the first listeners. Probably the most important source of John's imagery is the Old Testament. John draws much of his language from Old Testament Scripture, particularly the prophetic literature. For example, John's vision of the four horsemen in 6:1–12 draw on the horses from Zechariah 6:1–8. Both the trumpet (Rev 8–9) and bowl (16) plagues are modeled after the Exodus plagues (Exod 6–11). The image of the people of God as a bride adorned for her husband (Rev 21:9–21) also reflects Old Testament language that metaphorically compares the people of God to a bride (Isa 54:11–12; 61:10). The measuring of the New Jerusalem in 21:9–21 draws on the measuring of the temple in Ezekiel 40–48. Often the allusion to a specific Old Testament text in Revelation brings with it the larger context of the Old Testament allusion. Thus, when God (and Christ) are called the "alpha and omega, the first and the last, the beginning and end," the Old Testament background of this title is Isaiah 44:6 ("I am the first and I am the last. There is no God but me"), which is in the broader context of God's conflict with the false claims of idols (vv. 9–20). Such a context resonates in Revelation, where the readers are tempted to give allegiance to idolatrous Rome and its system of emperor worship. On the other hand, some of John's symbolism resonated with Greco-Roman background. While dragon-like figures, such as one finds in Revelation 12, played a role in the Old Testament and Jewish literature, they also featured in the mythology of the Greco-Roman world. The story of a dragon pursuing a woman about to give birth and then being thwarted in his attempts, so that the child flees, reflects Greco-Roman myths such as the Leto-Python-Apollo myth.[7] Likewise, images of famine and earthquakes would have been familiar to those living in the first-century Greco-Roman world.

---

7. Yarbro Collins, *Combat Myth*; Paul, *Revelation*, 214–15.

One important aspect of John's symbolism is the use of numbers. As with the rest of John's metaphorical language, numbers are not meant to be taken literally, or for the numerical values that they convey. They are not intended to be added up to calculate the timing of end-time events. Rather, they are important for their metaphorical and theological significance. Some important numbers and their symbolic significance in Revelation are the following:

> *Four.* The number four signifies the entire earth (e.g, the four corners of the earth).
>
> *Seven.* This is the most common number in Revelation, and as we have seen it also plays an important role as a structuring device. The number seven suggests perfection or completion.
>
> *Ten.* The number ten indicates completeness or wholeness. Its multiples (1000, 10,000) indicate a large, vast amount, a number of great magnitude.
>
> *Twelve.* This number, and its multiples (12 x 12 = 144), play a key role throughout Revelation, symbolizing the people of God. It is based on the twelve tribes of Israel and the twelve apostles.
>
> *3 ½ Years.* This temporal designation is half of seven, so it falls far short of perfection. Literally, it is "time, times, and half a time." It indicates a short, intense period of time that will be cut off and come to an end; it won't last forever.
>
> *42 months.* This is another way of referring to the same period of time as 3 ½ years. This number is based on the OT account of Israel's wandering in the wilderness (Num 3:3; Deut 8:2), and indicates a time of testing but also preservation.

1260 days. This is another way of designating the previous two time references: 1260 days = 42 months = 3 ½ years. These time periods are not to be added up, to get seven years or some other period of time; they are different ways of looking at the same period of time, the time of the church's testing and persecution.

1000 years. This designation of time does not communicate a literal period of time of 1000 years, but indicates a large, complete number (10 x 10 x 10) that far exceeds the previous three temporal designations for the churches persecution (3 ½ years, 42 months, 1260 days).

666. Probably the most well-known number is 666 found in Revelation 13:18. There are a couple of possibilities for understanding the significance of this number. First, it could be a number that falls short of the perfect number 777.[8] It is the number of humanity, and falls short of God's standards. Second, the number 666 could also reflect the name "Nero Caesar," when it is transliterated from Greek into Hebrew, and then the numerical values of the Hebrew letters are added up (666).[9] That is, the Christian audience is to see their situation as a sort of "return of a new Nero." The situation they face is to be perceived as if this evil emperor (Nero) is now embodied in the current ruling emperor (Domitian), to show the present emperor's true colors.

The point is to recognize that even the numbers used throughout Revelation, and even the temporal

8. See Mounce, *Revelation*, 265.

9. This practice of adding up the numerical value of ancient letters of the alphabet is known as *gematria*. See Bauckham, *Climax of Prophecy*, 384–407.

designations, are not communicating literal numerical values or measures of time, but instead communicating important symbolic and theological meaning.

John's symbols, then, are meant to describe reality, but not in a literal way. They work together in Revelation to form a "symbolic world" that the reader is invited to enter and experience. It is a world that is meant to portray an alternative view of this world. But these symbols are not to be decoded into literal descriptions of people, places, and events. They are meant to tell us something about the world in which the readers live. The symbols that Revelation contains should "be read for their theological meaning and power to evoke response."[10] Thus, the plague sequence of the trumpets (chs. 8–9) and bowls (ch. 16) appear to be modeled on the Exodus plagues, as already noted above. However, it is not the nature of the symbolism to allow us to translate them into exactly what the judgments will look like when they happen in history. Instead, what is more important is the theological meaning and response they powerfully evoke. God will certainly pour out his judgments (whatever they look like) on this evil world system (e.g., Rome) in the same way that he did on Egypt in the Exodus, and careful listeners will be keen to avoid being subject to this judgment by following the Lamb in obedience and disassociating from the evil world system that God is going to judge. This meaning takes priority over any attempts to identify precisely what the judgments will look like in history.[11]

---

10. Bauckham, *Theology of Revelation*, 20.

11. The main thing to avoid is matching the plagues up with modern-day realities and phenomena.

Revelation: Story, Structure, and Symbols

REFLECTION

1. Do you find it helpful to characterize Revelation as a story rather than just an indiscriminate collection of visions? Do you find it helpful to distinguish between Revelation's own story world and the reality to which it refers?

2. Have you read Revelation in its entirety before? Have you noted some of the connections and connecting devices noted in this chapter? What other connections between Revelation's visions stick out to you?

3

THE MESSAGES FROM THE RISEN LORD TO SEVEN CHURCHES (REVELATION 1–3)

INTRODUCTION TO REVELATION 1

THE FIRST CHAPTER OF the book of Revelation has much to say about the way that John's book is meant to be read. It sets the reader's expectation for what he/she will find in the subsequent chapters. Many commentators refer to all or part of chapter 1 as a prologue.[1] Whatever we label it precisely, it is important to emphasize that this chapter is not an unrelated afterthought to be skipped over to get to the main contents of the book. Rather, this chapter plays

---

1. Mounce, *Revelation*, 63; Schüssler Fiorenza, *Revelation: Vision of a Just World*, 39.

a crucial role in orienting the reader to what kind of book this is, how it is to be read, what the reader can expect to find in it, and how the reader should respond. So we would do well to slow down and read it carefully.

THE BOOK OF REVELATION ORIGINATES FROM GOD

The very first verse tells us that the source of this book is a revelation of Jesus Christ that has its ultimate origin in God himself (v. 1). By calling his work a "revelation," John places his book in a category of writings that communicates a visionary experience. The intent of his work is to uncover or unveil divine truth and knowledge that can come by no other means than a direct revelation from God. The phrase "revelation of Jesus Christ" is ambiguous. In both Greek and English it could imply either a revelation that is *about* Jesus Christ (Jesus is the object of the revealing) or a revelation that comes *from* Jesus Christ (Jesus is the subject of the revealing). Some commentators opt for both. However, the second is the most likely option: Jesus is the subject or source of the act of revealing. The revelation comes through Jesus Christ. This is made clear by the fact that John is setting up a "chain of revelation" in these verses. God → Jesus Christ → Angel → John (servants). Though Jesus Christ is the object or content of much of the rest of Revelation, there are plenty of sections in Revelation that are about other things besides Jesus Christ, making the first option above (Jesus is the object or content of the revelation) unlikely. That Jesus is to "show" it to his servants supports this. This statement of the revelatory chain adds authority to John's message. It is not his own, but comes to him through an act of revealing from Jesus Christ, and ultimately God himself. Angels also play a key role in Revelation, where they are responsible for the judgments and also interpret part of John's vision.

THE BOOK OF REVELATION IS ABOUT THINGS THAT WILL SOON TAKE PLACE

What Revelation reveals is the things that must take place soon (v. 1). This expression reflects Daniel 2:28: "what will happen in the last days." Instead of in the "last days," John sees these things as happening "soon." John sees the end time events of Daniel (and other Old Testament prophecies) as already being fulfilled in the person of Jesus Christ. With the death and resurrection of Jesus the last days have already been inaugurated, so the events Revelation speaks about are already being fulfilled. As John will say in v. 3, the "time is near." Revelation is not about events in the distant future (the twenty-first century, or any other century), but about events being fulfilled in the first readers' own day. Furthermore, even the events surrounding the second coming of Christ at the end of history are "soon" in the sense that John shares the perspective of other New Testament writers: the coming of Christ is near. Since the end has already been inaugurated at the first coming of Christ, his second coming to bring history to its close could happen at any time.

THE BOOK OF REVELATION IS A PROPHECY

Twice in v. 3 John refers to his work as a prophecy. By labeling his work a prophecy John reinforces that he is communicating the very words of God. Like his Old Testament prophetic predecessors, John will communicate messages from God of salvation and judgment. As we have already seen, the primary feature of prophetic literature is not that it predicts the future, although it does that (see Revelation 19–22), but that it announces a message of warning and encouragement to the readers.[2] As such, it requires a response of obedience from its hearers.

THE BOOK OF REVELATION IS TO BE OBEYED

Verse 3 indicates something about how the book of Revelation was first received. It pronounces a blessing on the one who reads and those who hear the book. That is, the book of Revelation would have been communicated orally to its first readers. But the blessing promised here is not for those who only hear the book read, but for those who keep it. To "keep" the words of Revelation means to obey it. This blessing in v. 3 is balanced out in the end of the book with a curse upon the one who hears the book but does not obey it (22:18–19). Ultimately, John's entire book calls for a response of obedience on the part of his listeners.

THE BOOK OF REVELATION IS A LETTER ADDRESSED TO SEVEN HISTORICAL CHURCHES

In v. 4 John indicates that he has chosen the form of a letter in which to communicate his words of prophecy to his readers. This verse constitutes a typical epistolary opening, such as one would find in one of Paul's letters. John identifies himself as the author, and then identifies his readers—seven historical churches in the ancient Roman province of Asia Minor. As a letter, Revelation will address directly the needs of these seven churches (see Rev 2–3). Therefore, as a letter it will communicate a message that will make sense to the first hearers/readers. Although John addresses

2. Ngundu, "Revelation," 1572.

seven actual churches in historical Asia, the number seven has symbolic significance, indicating the entire, complete or universal church of Jesus Christ.

THE BOOK OF REVELATION REMINDS THE READERS OF THE TRUE SOURCE OF THEIR SALVATION AND WELL-BEING

The epistolary greeting is expanded in vv. 4–6 with a Trinitarian reference. Rather than the Roman Empire and its emperor, the true source of the readers' peace and salvation comes first through the One who is truly sovereign over all things. God is first described as "the One who is, who was, and who is to come." This designation indicates God's eternity, as the one who has no beginning and end, who stands at the beginning and end of time, and who is coming in the future. The second reference is to seven Spirits. Most likely, within the context of the reference to God and to Jesus Christ, this is to be understood as a reference to the Holy Spirit. Seven as the number of completion or perfection suggests the complete manifestation and fullness of the Holy Spirit. Third, John refers to Jesus in terms of what he accomplished in his earthly life ("faithful witness"), his resurrection ("firstborn from the dead"), and his current sovereign rule ("ruler of the kings of the earth"). And in v. 6 Jesus is the one who through his death has enacted God's plan for redeeming his people to be his kings and priests. As God's priests in this world, God's people are to witness to the reality of God's kingdom and rule in the world.

The Messages from the Risen Lord

REVELATION PROMISES THAT GOD WILL BRING HISTORY TO ITS CONCLUSION WITH THE COMING OF JESUS

Verse 7 considers the further implication of Christ's lordship, death, and resurrection. Jesus Christ, who is the sovereign ruler of all, and who has already begun God's plan of redemption through his death on the cross (vv. 5-6) will bring God's redemptive plan to its conclusion with his future return to earth, in fulfillment of the Old Testament promises (v. 7). This promise is a combined quotation from Daniel 7:13 and Zechariah 12:10. Daniel 7:13 speaks of the Son of Man who comes on the clouds, and Zechariah 12:10 refers to a time when God will restore his people Israel and the world will look at the One (God) whom they have pierced. Both texts are now applied to Jesus and anticipate Christ's (second) coming in both salvation and judgment. A concluding reference to God assures the reader that the God who stands at the beginning and end of history (the "alpha and omega") and who is sovereign over all things guarantees that this promise of the coming of Christ will come to pass (v. 8).[3]

REVELATION IS WRITTEN BY JOHN WHO IS COMMISSIONED BY THE RISEN CHRIST TO ADDRESS THE CHURCHES

Revelation 1:9-20 constitutes a commissioning of John as a prophet in an inaugural vision to receive this revelation and communicate it to the seven churches in Asia Minor (1:4). The heart of the section is a vision of the heavenly, exalted Christ, who commissions John to write this vision

---

3. Schüssler Fiorenza, *Revelation: Vision of a Just World*, 44.

and send it to the churches. Verse 9 situates the scene for the vision relationally, by demonstrating John's solidarity with his readers, introducing key themes to be developed in the rest of the book: the presence of God's kingdom, yet not without tribulation and the need for endurance. The vision is also situated geographically on the island of Patmos, where John likely is banished because of his preaching the Word of God. The vision is then situated temporally (v. 10) as taking place on the "Lord's Day," most likely a term for Sunday, the first day of the week when the churches met for worship in celebration of Christ's resurrection.

The remainder of the chapter constitutes John's inaugural vision of the risen, exalted Lord (vv. 10–20). John hears a voice that commands him to write what he is about to see and send it to the seven churches in Asia Minor. This is a commissioning scene similar to other Old Testament prophets, such as Isaiah and Ezekiel (Isa 6; Ezek 1–2). When John turns around to look at who was speaking to him, he sees a vision of the Son of Man seated on his throne in all his glory. The vision begins by stating the relationship between the Son of Man and the golden lampstands that John sees (vv. 12–13). In v. 20 Jesus himself will make clear that the seven lampstands correspond to the seven churches of Asia. Jesus is present in the midst of his churches, and he is their sovereign Lord and judge. The careful reader will note that each of the seven messages to the churches in chapters 2–3 begins with a reference to Christ taken from 1:10–20 which is relevant to the situation of the church being addressed. As the Son of Man, Jesus is present with his churches and now evaluates them. The vision of the Son of Man consists of a kaleidoscope of images taken primarily from the Old Testament. The image of the lampstand comes from the temple, and is found in Zechariah 4:2–6. The application to the churches suggests that they are God's temple and are to represent and witness to God's presence in the world. The description of Christ primarily draws on the heavenly Son of Man from Daniel 7 and 10. The clothing imagery of the long robe and sash portrays Christ as a priestly and kingly figure, whose role is to exercise oversight of the lampstands by evaluating them, either commending and encouraging them or rebuking and warning them.[4] This is reinforced by the description of his white hair and eyes blazing like fire. He takes on the divine qualities of the Ancient of Days from Daniel 7:9, and his blazing eyes point to his ability to see with discrimination what is going on in his churches. His feet like glowing bronze (v. 15) further point to his power and stability. He also holds the seven stars, which v. 20 will interpret as symbolic of the seven angels over the seven churches (see chs. 2–3). The fact that he holds them suggests his sovereignty and control over the churches. The sharp double-edged sword protruding from his mouth is clearly an image of judgment. Thus, the entire vision portrays Christ as the sovereign ruler and judge who is present with his church and will evaluate it as its sovereign Lord.

John's response is common in other apocalyptic visionary texts: at the sight of the risen Christ he falls down as if dead (v. 17). Christ's response to John indicates the basis for his role as the exalted king and judge: his sovereignty over history ("first and last"), which is a result of his defeat of death through his resurrection (v. 18). Based on the fact that Christ has been installed as the exalted Son of Man who functions as king and judge which is based on his defeat of death through his resurrection, Christ now has the authority to address his churches, and so he commissions John to write. The content of what he is to write in v. 19 is

---

4. Beale, *Revelation*, 208.

ambiguous: is the command to write threefold, "what you saw (past), what is now (present), and what will take place later (future)"? Or is it twofold, "what you see (referring to the entire book), that is, what is and what will take place"? Whatever the case, it is illegitimate to see this as outlining a chronological sequence of events corresponding to specific sections of Revelation. The formula in v. 19 refers to the entire book of Revelation, and throughout will refer to events in the readers own day and in the future. The scene is now set for John to address the seven churches through the authority of the risen and exalted Christ.

JESUS ADDRESSES THE SEVEN CHURCHES IN ASIA MINOR THROUGH HIS PROPHET, JOHN (CHS. 2–3)

Revelation 2–3 is important because these chapters provide the historical backdrop for understanding the rest of Revelation. Chapters 4–22 will, in the form of an apocalyptic vision, repeat and reinforce the messages to the churches in chapters 2–3. A couple of observations need to be made about Jesus' address to the seven churches in 2–3. First, though it is common to label these as letters, they are more accurately characterized as prophetic messages. Hence, they will function as a prophetic critique of the people of God, either encouraging or warning them. Second, only two of the churches are suffering any kind of persecution and are marginalized (Smyrna, Philadelphia). The other five are guilty of some kind of compromise or complacency with Rome. It is important to understand that the persecution suffered by Christians was not an official, empire-wide phenomenon, but was local and sporadic. It took the form of things like slander, ostracism, and poverty as results of refusal to participate in the imperial economy—all things they needed to overcome. Though it was a likelihood, martyrdom was not yet the norm, and John knows of only one person so far (Antipas in 2:13) who has died for his faithful witness. Third, the messages are addressed to the angels of the churches. In Revelation angels are always references to heavenly, angelic beings, not human beings. Most likely the angels are the heavenly representatives of the earthly churches. In apocalyptic literature, earthly entities often have heavenly counterparts. Fourth, as already mentioned, each message begins with an identification of the exalted Christ taken from the description of the Son of Man in 1:10–20 which is relevant to each church's situation. Furthermore, each message ends with a promise to the church, if they overcome, taken from the final eschatological vision of Revelation 20–22. Finally, these seven churches existed on a circular route of travel, beginning with Ephesus and ending with Laodicea. Moreover, they probably represented the kinds of issues that all of the churches in that region faced. Many of them were hotbeds of emperor worship, or other pagan centers of worship.

Jesus, to the Church in Ephesus (2:1–7)

The first church that Jesus addresses through John with a prophetic message is the church located in Ephesus, probably the most prominent of the cities to which John writes. It was an important commercial center, hosted a temple to the goddess Artemis, and was an important center of the emperor cult. Jesus identifies himself to the church as the one holding the seven stars in his hand and who walks in the midst of the seven lampstands (churches) from 1:13, 16. Therefore, Christ knows what the church faces, but he is also able to see its faults. Like some of the other messages, Christ begins with a note of praise: the Ephesian church is to be commended for enduring hardships, and they have worked hard. They have also refused to tolerate falsehood, as shown by resisting those who falsely claim to be apostles (2:2–3). They further have resisted the false teaching of a group that John calls the Nicolaitans, who were probably teaching Christians to accommodate to the pagan Roman world.[5] But all is not well with the church. Christ has one thing against them: they have lost their first love. The text is ambiguous as to who the object of their love is. God, or fellow Christians? Most likely it refers to their loss of being zealous in their love for God and Christ, which has resulted in lack of witness. The readers are commanded to repent and return to their first love. Therefore, the readers are called upon to listen to the message carefully and respond in obedience. The reward for obeying the call to repent is a share in the tree of life and paradise of God, both metaphors for eternal life that anticipate the final vision in 22:1–2.

Jesus, to the Church in Smyrna (2:8–11)

Smyrna is one of the only two churches that receives an exclusively positive evaluation by Christ. Jesus identifies himself as the "first and the last" and the one who rose from the dead, appropriate descriptions for a church that is suffering ostracism and persecution and which is called to be faithful even to the point of death. First, Christ contrasts their physical poverty with their spiritual wealth. Their poverty may be the result of refusal to participate in the Roman imperial economy. Second, Christ identifies

5. Koester, *Revelation and the End of All Things*, 62.

the source of their trouble as hostility from the Jewish Synagogue, who are perhaps slandering the Christians before the governing authorities. Third, John calls their synagogue the "synagogue of Satan." Most likely John is identifying the true source behind their persecution: it ultimately comes from Satan himself (see Revelation 12). Fourth, John encourages the church by limiting their suffering to ten days. This is most likely not to be interpreted as a reference to ten literal days, but symbolically indicates a significant, but short and limited period of time of persecution. It probably has its background in the ten days of testing of Daniel's three friends in Daniel 1:12–16.[6] As a reward for their faithfulness, the church is promised the crown of life, which is a metaphor for eternal life, and protection from the second death, which is promised at the end of the book in 20:6 (see 20:14; 21:8).

Jesus, to the Church in Pergamum (2:12–17)

The city of Pergamum was a capital city, was home to temples to pagan gods, such as Zeus, and was a center for emperor worship. Christ begins by identifying himself as the one with the sword coming out of his mouth from 1:16. This suggests that Christ's primary posture towards the church in Pergamum is one of judgment. Like most of the other messages, Christ's begins with a positive evaluation. The Christians in Pergamum live in the midst of Satan's throne, probably a reference to pagan influence and emperor worship in the city. Yet they have not denied Christ, even though one person (Antipas) among them has paid the ultimate price of his life because of remaining faithful to his witness for Christ (v. 13). Yet commendation turns

6. Beale, *Revelation*, 242–43.

quickly to censure. Some in the church follow the teaching of Balaam, a name from the Old Testament (Num 22–24) that John uses to characterize a teaching that probably promotes compromise with the pagan environment and Roman Empire. Balaam led Israel astray to commit idolatry and immorality in Numbers, making him a fitting exemplar of the teaching John combats here. The act of eating meat sacrificed to idols probably refers to eating meat in the context of the Roman religious celebrations, so that the problem was assimilation to Roman idolatrous religious practices. The church also has some who follow the teaching of the Nicolaitans, a group also teaching that compromise with pagan Rome is compatible with their Christian faith. Christ calls the church to repent of this so that they will not be subject to Christ's judgment (ultimately 19:15). If they repent and refuse to compromise, Christ will give them the hidden manna and a white stone. The manna is a symbol of eschatological life taken from the manna given to Israel in the wilderness, and the white stone may have suggested entrance to a banquet or a vote of acquittal.[7] Together, both refer to eternal life and entrance into their heavenly inheritance in 21:1—22:5.

Jesus, to the Church in Thyatira (2:18–29)

To the church in the city of Thyatira, Jesus identifies himself as having flaming eyes and feet like bronze from 1:14–15. This suggests that Jesus addresses the church as the one who is able to see and penetrate into their hearts and is strong and stable. Jesus begins by commending the church for their love, faithfulness, service, and endurance. Yet Jesus also unveils a problem: they tolerate a woman, a

7. Witherington, *Revelation*, 103-4.

prophetess, named Jezebel. Most likely she is also teaching that compromise with the Roman empire is permissible. Jezebel is probably not the prophetess's real name, but is the name John gives her based on her similarity to queen Jezebel in the Old Testament (1 Kgs 18–19), who led the Israelites into sexual immorality and idolatry. Again, the problem is accommodation with the pagan, Roman environment. To refuse to participate in occasions where meat offered to idols would have been eaten in the context of religious observances during meetings of associations (such as trade guilds) could have drastic social and economic consequences. Jesus has given this prophetess time to repent, but she has refused. The graphic language of throwing her into a sick bed, and those who associate with her, and striking her children dead, demonstrates the seriousness of the situation and God's judgment upon the sin of rebellion against Christ and his word. The goal of the judgment is repentance. But Christ returns to commendation of those in the church who refuse to follow this teaching, which he also calls the deep things of Satan. The prophetess may have been claiming to teach the deep things of God, but now John says that in reality it is the "deep things of Satan" she is teaching, in that the teaching persuades Christians to compromise their faithful witness to Christ by accommodating pagan culture and activities. If the Thyatiran Christians overcome and refuse to compromise, they are promised a share in Christ's rule, in fulfillment of Psalm 2:9, a promise that anticipates the rule of the saints with Christ in 20:4–6 and 22:5.

Jesus, to the Church in Sardis (3:1–6)

Jesus identifies himself to the church in Sardis as the one who has the seven Spirits of God and holds the seven stars from 1:16. Both images point to Jesus' sovereignty and authority. Jesus has no words of commendation for the church in Sardis, but only rebuke. The church has a reputation of being alive, probably a reference to their prosperity and lack of affliction,[8] yet in reality they are dead in Christ's eyes. In other words, the church is Sardis is comfortable in its existence in the world, to the point that they are not aware that they are spiritually on the verge of death and void of witness. Using the image of sleep, Christ calls them to wake up out of their spiritual complacency and slumber. Repeating the words of the earthly Jesus (Matt 24:33), the message warns the church in Sardis of Christ coming to them as a thief, suggesting unexpectedness and unpreparedness if they do not wake up from their complacency. This coming is probably a reference to Christ coming in judgment at the end of history in 19:11–21. Still, there are some who have not defiled their clothing, a metaphor for purity. This suggests that there are many others who have compromised through accommodation with pagan Rome. If the Christians in Sardis overcome by waking up from their complacency and remaining pure from the influence of the pagan world, they will one day receive white robes, a symbol of purity and eschatological salvation (19:8–9; see 7:9). Also, God will not erase their names from the book of life, that is, he will keep them until the end, a promise also found in the eschatological final vision (20:12, 14), and acknowledge them before the Father.

Jesus, to the Church in Philadelphia (3:7–13)

The church at Philadelphia is the only other church, along with Smyrna, to receive an exclusively positive evaluation

---

8. Koester, *Revelation and the End of All Things*, 71.

by the risen Christ. Jesus' relationship to the church in Philadelphia is described as the one who holds the keys of David and has the authority to open and shut. This imagery comes from Isaiah 22, which refers to Israel's king, Eliakim, who is given the keys of the house of David. As the true son of David and king, Jesus is now given the keys of David. The keys and image of opening and closing suggest authority to give entrance into the kingdom of God. Likewise, the language of an "open door" is not an opportunity for mission or ministry, but entrance into the messianic kingdom. That is, Christ has the authority to grant entrance into his kingdom, a word of encouragement for a marginalized church with little power and suffering persecution. The fact that they have little power probably suggests they are small and poor. In the midst of their marginalized status, they have kept Jesus' name. The source of their trouble is again attributed to the Jewish synagogue (see also 2:9), most likely a conflict over who are the true people of God, and perhaps slandering them before governing authorities. In a play on words, Christ promises that because they have *kept* his word, he will *keep* them safe during the hour of testing that is coming on the world, probably the plagues to come in the rest of the book (chaps. 8–9, 16) or the final judgment (19). And if they overcome and remain faithful to the end, God promises them a place in the temple/New Jerusalem in 21:1—22:5.

Jesus, to the Church at Laodicea (3:14–22)

The final church that Jesus addresses with a prophetic message is the church in the city of Laodicea, the last city on the circuit. Christ identifies himself as the "Amen" and as the beginning of or ruler over God's creation. This self-identification refers to Jesus as the one who speaks the truth and who is sovereign over all creation, and perhaps over a new creation (see 21:1). The church in Laodicea receives no commendation, but only rebuke. The rebuke begins with an image of water temperature. This imagery of hot, cold, and lukewarm water and its associations needs to be understood from the context of the first-century readers in Laodicea. Most likely, the hot water would have recalled the hot mineral water springs from the nearby city of Hierapolis, with their healing properties. The cold water probably recalled the cold water found in nearby Colossae. Cold water was refreshing and valued for drinking. It is also possible that hot and cold recalled the hot drink or the cold drink that would have been served at a banquet, since this message ends with banquet imagery in v. 20. Whatever the exact background, hot and cold are both *positive* metaphors.[9] Lukewarm water may recall Laodicea's own water supply, which may have been less than ideal for drinking.[10] Or the background could be that lukewarm water was used to induce vomiting. In any case, lukewarm water was a negative metaphor, signifying uselessness. Lukewarm does not stand in-between hot and cold, but it stands opposite both hot and cold. Hot and cold both had positive connotations, and lukewarm had negative connotations. That is, lukewarm is not an image of indifference, indecision, or "middle of the road." It is an image of uselessness and worthlessness. Jesus wants the Laodiceans to be like the hot water and cold water in nearby cities—it is good for

9. Popular understandings that pit hot and cold against each other as opposites—spiritually hot and spiritually cold—are incorrect, and would not have been the associations made by readers in first-century Laodicea and its regions.

10. There is no evidence that Laodicea piped in water from another city because it lacked water, so that the water was lukewarm by the time it got there. Laodicea had its own water supply.

healing or refreshing to drink. Instead they are likewarm water—it is good for nothing but inducing vomiting.

The rest of Jesus' rebuke shows how the Laodiceans are lukewarm. The church has become wealthy and self-sufficient to the point that they do not need anything else: "I'm rich; I have become wealthy and need nothing" (v. 17). They have likely grown rich off the Roman economy and now no longer have need of Christ. Continuing the language of commerce, Christ says that although they are rich economically, they are poor spiritually. And he encourages them to buy true riches using images that probably reflect the products of their region: gold, clothes, and eye ointment. Jesus exhorts them to secure their spiritual counterparts to overcome their spiritual poverty (poor, naked, and blind). The result of their spiritual poverty and self-sufficiency is that Christ stands outside of the church. Using banquet imagery, Jesus exhorts the church to invite him into their midst once more to share in the banquet (see 19:7–9). Jesus promises the Laodicean church that if they overcome (by repenting of their self-sufficiency) he will grant them the right to sit with him on his throne and rule. This promise anticipates the eschatological rule of the saints with Christ in 20:4–6 and 22:5.

CONCLUSION

The messages to the seven churches reveal the true condition of the churches as evaluated by Jesus through his prophet, John. Most of the churches are affected by complacency and the temptation to compromise with the pagan Roman environment, and therefore are ineffective in their witness. Only two churches are suffering any kind of persecution and ostracism at the hands of local authorities. Depending on their situation, the churches will read

Revelation differently.[11] For those who are compromising and who have become complacent, Revelation will function as a warning to them to repent and avoid the judgments described in the rest of the book. For those (two) churches that are persecuted because they have remained faithful, Revelation will function as a message of hope and encouragement to endure and to remain faithful, no matter what the consequences, for they will be vindicated. In each of the messages, the readers are called upon to "listen to" the words of Jesus to the churches, which is identical to listening to the Spirit. To listen to the seven messages entails obeying what they say.[12]

REFLECTION

1. It is often concluded that New Testament authors did not realize they were writing Scripture at the time they were composing their books (e.g., Luke or Jude). Do you think this is true of John and the book of Revelation given what he says in chapter 1? Why or why not?

2. Why do you think so many of the churches had become comfortable and complacent living within the Roman Empire?

3. Which of the churches addressed in Revelation 2–3 most closely resembles the modern-day church? How would this make a difference in how Revelation should be read?

---

11. Culy, *Book of Revelation*.
12. Wilson, *Victory through the Lamb*, 40.

4

A VISION OF HEAVEN'S THRONE ROOM (REVELATION 4-5)

JOHN'S "VISION PROPER" BEGINS in 4:1 and extends through 22:5. It is important to recognize that chapters 4-22 do not refer to events and information that takes place chronologically after chapters 2-3. Rather, 4-22 cover the same ground temporally as 2-3. That is, they refer to the same time, events, persons, and places as 2-3, but now from the perspective of an apocalyptic vision. Chapters 2-3 could be seen as a more straightforward prophetic critique of the churches and their situation. Chapters 4-22 will now address the same churches and their time and situation, but in the form of an apocalyptic vision. Chapters 4-5 are foundational for the entire book of Revelation. The scene shifts from earth in chapters 2-3 now to heaven in 4:1. This section contains a vision of a heavenly throne room, where God and the Lamb are seated on the throne and are worshiped by all creation. As we have already seen, the rest of the book of Revelation tells the story of how this scene in heaven, where God and the Lamb are worshiped and their sovereignty acknowledged, becomes a reality on earth. Furthermore, chapters 4–5 provide a sense of divine sovereignty and control for the rest of the book. All the events, judgments, persecution of the people of God, and apparent chaos and disorder described in the rest of the book are under divine control. The world is not out of control, despite appearances, but is to be seen from the perspective of the heavenly throne room, a place of order and control.

At the heart of the vision is the question: Who is really in control of the universe? Who is worthy of worship and allegiance? John's vision provides an answer with God and the Lamb seated on the throne at the center of all things, receiving the praise and worship of all creation. The central image of chapters 4–5 is the throne. The word "throne" occurs nineteen times (seventeen referring to God's throne) in these two chapters alone. The throne is a political image, suggesting sovereignty and kingship. Chapters 4–5 draw primarily on similar heavenly throne room scenes found in Isaiah 6 and Ezekiel 1–2, but probably also draw on Roman imperial court scenes, where Caesar is on his throne, and his cohorts surround him and render him acclamation and allegiance. John's vision, then, would be a parody of the Roman court scene and will counter imperial claims. It is not Caesar who is at the center of the universe, in control of all things, and worthy of acclamation and worship. God's throne, not Caesar's, stands at the center of all reality. Only God and the Lamb who are sovereign over all things are worthy of worship.

A Vision of Heaven's Throne Room (Revelation 4–5)

Revelation 4–5 makes up one extended heavenly throne-room scene. Chapter 4 functions to provide the backdrop or to set the stage for the events that transpire in chapter 5. The vision is chapter 4 is static and descriptive of God's throne and its environs (in Greek there are almost no main verbs). Chapter 5 contains the main actions and events that take place, centered in the activity of the slaughtered Lamb. Revelation 4–5 is carefully integrated into John's overall vision. First, it connects back to chapters 1–3 with the mention of the same voice in 4:1 which spoke to John back in 1:10. Furthermore, the promise that concludes the messages to the seven churches—of Christ overcoming and sitting on the Father's throne—in 3:21 now gets picked up with the throne in chapters 4–5. Second, the image of the throne will play a key role in the rest of the book and occurs in several sections. The scroll in chapter 5 will provide the setting for the unleashing of the seven seals in chapters 6–8.

VISION OF THE ONE SITTING ON THE THRONE (CH. 4)

John begins this section with the preparation for the vision. A door in heaven stands opened, an open heaven being a common motif for having a visionary experience in apocalyptic writings (Ezek 1:1; 1 Enoch 14:15; 2 Baruch 22:1; Testament of Levi 5:1; Apocalypse of Paul, 21:24–28). A heavenly voice summons John to come up to heaven for the purpose of seeing a vision. What John is told is that he will be shown what will take place "after these things." This phrase should probably be understood similar to 1:1 ("what must take place soon") and 3 ("the time is near"). John will be shown what is already taking place with the coming of Christ to inaugurate the future end-time promises from the Old Testament.

The One Seated on the Throne (4:2–3, 5–6a)

John begins by describing what is at the center of his vision, the throne of God. As seen above, the throne is a symbol of God's sovereignty and rule over the entire cosmos, and is a challenge to all earthly thrones, including Rome. Everything else revolves around or issues from God's throne. All reality is oriented toward the center, displacing Rome from the center of all things.[1] John does not describe God's visible form directly, but describes his radiant appearance, likening God's appearance to three precious jewels: jasper, ruby, and a rainbow like an emerald (NIV). The importance of these stones is that they signify divine glory and splendor and God's presence. The first stone, jasper, will again occur in the description of the new creation/New Jerusalem in 21:11, suggesting that chapter 4 anticipates the final vision where God's heavenly presence finally fills the entire creation. John creates a picture of God's glorious and radiant splendor that in one sense is beyond description. John moves out from the center to describe what is around or adjacent to the throne. John describes lightning and thunder coming from the throne, and there are seven lamps burning before the throne which John identifies as the seven Spirits of God (see 1:4). Also there is a sea of glass before it (vv. 5–6). These images convey a sense of God's power and holiness, that his throne cannot be approached lightly, and that he is transcendent and separate from his creation. The lightning and thunder also convey God's judgments, since this image gets picked up later in

---

1. Bauckham, *Theology of Revelation*, 33.

A Vision of Heaven's Throne Room (Revelation 4–5)

Revelation in connection with God's seal (8:5), trumpet (11:19), and bowl judgments (16:18–21).[2] All the judgments that take place in the rest of Revelation issue from the throne and are an outworking of God's holiness and sovereignty. The sea of glass like crystal is also drawn from Ezekiel 1:22. The sea in Revelation usually has negative connotations, emblematic of chaos and evil and the realm of the dead (13:1; 20:13; 21:1). But here it is calmed and tame, under the sovereign control of God.

The Heavenly Attendants and Their Praise (4:4, 6b–11)

Encircling the throne of God are twenty-four other thrones with twenty-four elders seated on them (v. 4). The precise identity of the elders is uncertain. Do they refer to people or to angelic beings? John describes them as wearing white garments and possessing crowns, elsewhere descriptions of the people of God in Revelation (2:10; 3:4–5, 18, 21; 6:11; 19:8), and they sit on thrones, a promise made to the people of God (3:21–22; 20:4–6). Most likely they are angelic beings who make up the heavenly council, like the four living creatures, and the number twenty-four may come from adding up twelve and twelve, the twelve tribes of Israel and the twelve apostles of the Lamb (see 21:12–14). These heavenly beings would then be the heavenly representatives of the saints on earth, hence their wearing white garments and crowns, and sitting on thrones.[3] They function as divine attendants to the throne in John's vison, and they worship God (vv. 10–11).

John then turns his attention to another heavenly group standing near the throne: four living creatures (vv.

2. Bauckham, *Theology of Revelation*, 42.
3. Beale, *Revelation*, 322.

6b–8). The four living creatures all share the feature of having eyes covering them and wings, features which identify them with the angelic beings in Ezekiel 1:5–14 and Isaiah 6:2. Furthermore, each living creature is identified with a specific animal—lion, ox, eagle—except the third one is said to have the face of a human (v. 7). The most likely identification of these four living creatures is that they are angelic beings who represent in heaven the entirety of life in the created order (four is a number symbolizing creation). Their primary function is to render God ceaseless worship, which they do day and night (v. 8). The hymn that John hears them sing serves to interpret the significance of the heavenly throne room vision. The hymn consists of a threefold designation for God as "Holy, holy, holy" (from Isa 6:3), "the Lord God Almighty," and "the One who was and is and is to come." The first two designations serve to emphasize the transcendence and sovereignty of God over his creation and over history. The third designation describes God as eternal (see also 1:8), standing at the beginning and end of his creation, and coming in the future to bring judgment and salvation.[4]

The final component in the initial throne room scene is the worship by the twenty-four elders in vv. 9–11. John tells us that whenever the four living creatures give glory, honor, and thanksgiving to the one sitting on the throne, then the twenty-four elders will fall down before the throne and worship. This could refer to the previous verse (v. 8). It is also possible that it anticipates other places in the rest of Revelation where the elders fall down along with the four living creatures and worship in response to Gods judgment (7:1; 19:4). Most likely, this refers to 5:13–14, since this is where the elders fall down before the

---

4. Bauckham, *Theology of Revelation*, 29–30.

A Vision of Heaven's Throne Room (Revelation 4–5)

throne and worship. The hymn in v. 11 ascribes worthiness to God to receive glory, honor, and power. The reason he is worthy is stated in the second half of the hymn: because God is the sovereign creator of all things; to him all things owe their existence. Again, the hymn serves to interpret the significance of the vision of chapter 4. God is worthy of worship because he is the sovereign creator of all that exists, and therefore rules over it. Furthermore, this vision functions as a counterclaim to Imperial Roman rule. It is not the Caesar who is in control of the world and the sovereign ruler worthy of worship, but only God who is seated in heaven at the center of the cosmos.

After examining some of the details of this vision, it is helpful to step back and get an overall impression of the vision as a whole. The reader gets the impression of God seated in heaven far above his creation in all his splendor and majesty. God's will and sovereignty are perfectly acknowledged in all heaven, a place of order and beauty. This scene is meant to evoke a sense of awe and mystery, and moves the reader to the true center of reality and the true object of worship. For those churches suffering persecution and marginalization, this vision of God on the throne would be an encouragement that God is in sovereign control and will return to bring judgment and salvation. But for those churches which are compromising and complacent, the vision of God seated on his throne as ruler and judge would be disturbing. But chapter 4 is only the setting or backdrop for the main events that take place in chapter 5.

VISION OF THE SLAIN LAMB WHO TAKES THE SCROLL (CH. 5)

In contrast to the more static scene in chapter 4, the throne room now becomes a place of movement and activity.

Several key elements from the scene in chapter 4 carry over into chapter 5: the throne and the one seated on it, the four living creatures, the twenty-four elders, the seven Spirits of God, hymns sung in praise. Yet chapter 5 will introduce new characters and features into the heavenly throne room vision. The scene opens with the one sitting on the throne, but now John introduces the reader to the first new feature in his vision: a scroll in God's right hand (v. 1). The scroll appears to be an *opisthograph*, a scroll written on both sides, and John draws this feature from Ezekiel's vision where Ezekiel sees a scroll written on both sides (Ezek 2:9–10). In Ezekiel, the scroll contains "words of lamentation, mourning, and woe" (v. 10), that is, a message of judgment. Most likely, John's scroll contains God's plan for bringing about judgment but also salvation to the world. It contains God's plan for implementing his rule and sovereignty on earth, which is already acknowledged in heaven in chapter 4. The scroll is sealed so that its contents are hidden. John introduces another figure in v. 2, an angel who in a loud voice raises a question. The question introduces a dilemma that forms the main point of the narrative: "Who is worthy to open the scroll and break its seals?" This is necessary so that the contents of the book can be divulged and set in motion, since they are presently sealed, and thus hidden. Verse 3 may suggest that it is the angel who searches for someone worthy to open the book, or it could imply that John himself searched for someone to open the book. The extent of his search is made clear with the threefold geographical reference to heaven, earth, and under the earth. In other words, the search left no stone unturned, but nothing and no one in creation was found worthy to open and look into the book. To look into the book is more than just reading it and seeing its

A Vision of Heaven's Throne Room (Revelation 4–5)

contents, but refers to actually divulging and enacting the contents. John responds by weeping, since what is at stake is the fulfilling of God's plan of redemption and justice for the whole world as contained in the scroll.

One of the twenty-four elders from 4:4 responds to John's weeping with the solution. This solution is revealed in two stages. First, John *hears* the voice of one of the elders (v. 5), who introduces a figure that he describes with Old Testament, Davidic language. This will be no ordinary, human figure, since a search has already been made throughout the entirety of creation and created beings, with no one being found worthy. This figure that the elder introduces is the Lion from the tribe of Judah, a description that comes from Genesis 49:9–10, which portrays the tribe of Judah as a lion's whelp that is promised a scepter. The second phrase, the root of David, comes from Isaiah 11:1, which anticipates a Davidic ruler who will strike the earth (v. 4). Together, these descriptive titles portray a powerful, majestic figure who is a messianic ruler and who has conquered, presumably in military fashion. However, when John turns around to look at this figure, he *sees* instead a slain Lamb (v. 6). This is part of John's "hear"/"see" dialectic found at several places throughout Revelation (see ch. 7 below): John "hears" a lion from the tribe of Judah, a Davidic ruler, but what he "sees" is a slaughtered Lamb. These are not two different figures, but both refer to the same person, Jesus Christ. The two images mutually interpret each other. Jesus is a mighty, Davidic warrior, but he is victorious paradoxically through his suffering and sacrificial death. Thus, John redefines power. The image of the Lamb describes precisely how the Lion of the tribe of Judah will conquer: it is through the death of Christ that he defeats evil and purchases people to be a kingdom of priests (1:5-6; 5:9). This will also provide a model for how Jesus' followers are to overcome, which they are called to do in the seven messages to the churches in chapters 2-3: faithful witness in suffering and even death. The Lamb is further described as having seven horns and seven eyes, which are identified as the seven Spirits of God sent into all the earth. That is, the Lamb possesses power and sovereignly sees and knows all things. He will accomplish his purposes throughout the world. It is through this fullness of divine power represented by the seven Spirits that the Lamb will be victorious throughout the world.[5] Jesus' status as Messianic ruler, but as one who suffers and dies, qualifies him to open the scroll and divulge its contents, God's plan for judgment and salvation.

The climax of the scene in Revelation 5 is reached in v. 7, where the slaughtered Lamb approaches the throne and takes the scroll from the hand of the one seated on the throne, in response to the dilemma foregrounded in the angel's question in v. 2. The rest of the chapter is a series of hymns sung in praise to the Lamb (and God) that celebrate this event of taking the scroll in v. 7. Like chapter 4, the hymns sung here function to interpret the significance of the event of taking the scroll in vv. 1-7. There is an important literary structure in the presentation of the hymns narrated in this section. The activity of worship of God and the Lamb moves out from the throne in widening concentric circles: first the four living creatures and twenty-four elders sing praise (vv. 8-10), then the voice of many angels (vv. 11-12), and finally every creature throughout the entire cosmos (v. 13). The focus of all of these hymns is the worthiness of the Lamb as God's agent to take the scroll

---

5. Bauckham, *Theology of Revelation*, 109.

A Vision of Heaven's Throne Room (Revelation 4–5)

and set its contents into motion, which he does because as the Messiah he has suffered and died for his people.

The first hymn is sung by the four living creatures and twenty-four elders (vv. 8–10). Before their song is recorded, John says that they are holding golden bowls full of incense, which he identifies as the prayers of the saints. The prayers of the saints are probably to be identified with those from the fifth seal later in 6:9–11, and in the introduction to the trumpet judgments in 8:3–5, which were prayers of God's people for vindication and judgment of their enemies. The reference to the prayers here in 5:8 suggests that the Lamb's work of his sacrificial death praised here provides the answer to the prayers of God's people for justice and vindication from their persecutors.[6] The hymn celebrates the worthiness of the Lamb to take the scroll (see v. 7) and divulge its contents precisely because he was slaughtered, and as a result of his sacrificial death has redeemed a transcultural people (from every tribe, language, people, and nation) to be the people of God. The language of "slain Lamb" and "redemption" recalls the Exodus, where the Passover lamb made possible the liberation of God's people from Egypt. In the same way Christ enacts a new Exodus in liberating his people from bondage to sin through his own sacrificial death.[7] Repeating the reference to Christ's work in 1:5–6, this act of redemption makes the people a kingdom and priests in fulfillment of Exodus 19:6. John takes language from the Old Testament that applied to Israel and now applies it to the new people of God from every tribe and nation (not just Israel). This new people will form a community that as God's kingdom and priests would boldly embody God's kingdom and presence in the

---

6. Beale, *Revelation*, 357.

7. Schüssler Fiorenza, *Revelation: Vision of a Just World*, 61.

world in bringing the heavenly scene in Revelation 4–5 to earth. They will "enact" the heavenly scene in chapters 4–5, where God's sovereignty and rule are perfectly realized and acknowledged, by witnessing to his rule and presence on earth and worshiping God alone. The promise that they will reign upon the earth finds its fulfillment in 20:4–6, but it is in the new creation that their role as a kingdom and priests finds its ultimate fulfillment (22:3–5).

Broadening out in a wider concentric circle, the next hymn evoked by the act of the Lamb taking the scroll in v. 7 is sung by an incalculable host of angels (thousands upon thousands, ten thousands upon ten thousands) in vv. 11–12. The angelic hosts declare the Lamb's worthiness to receive "power and wealth and wisdom and strength and honor and glory and praise" (v. 12) recalling the act of "receiving" the scroll (v. 7). The seven-fold ascription of worthiness reflects the praise given to God in 4:11 now given to the Lamb. The reason the Lamb is worthy is indicated in the first line: his sacrificial death that accomplishes God's plan of judgment and redemption has made him worthy to release the contents of the scroll.

The final hymn is the largest concentric circle from the throne sung by every creature in heaven, earth, and under the earth (v. 13; see v. 3), anticipating the universal worship in chapter 21. Now God and the Lamb both occupy the single throne and equally receive "praise and honor and glory and power." Yet for John this does not violate his monotheistic stance that only God can be worshiped (19:10; 22:9). Jesus occupies the same throne as God and receives the exact same praise because Christ shares in the very identity and being of God. Christ clearly stands on the God-the-Creator (4:11) side of the Creator/creature divide, as demonstrated by the fact that he is not included

A Vision of Heaven's Throne Room (Revelation 4–5)

in the "heaven, earth, and under the earth" of vv. 3, 13. In fulfillment of 4:9–11, the heavenly worship scene concludes with the four living creatures worshiping and the elders falling down.

CHAPTERS 4–5 AND THE BOOK OF REVELATION

The stage is now set for the rest of Revelation's story. God is seated on his throne in heaven, and God's sovereignty and will are perfectly acknowledged in heaven. The only thing that remains is for the heavenly scene in chapter 4 to become a reality on earth. In chapter 5 John narrates how this will take place. How will God's sovereignty and will which are perfectly realized in heaven finally transpire on earth, which presently contradicts it in the form of the Roman Empire? The initial answer is that Jesus Christ, through his sacrificial death, is worthy to open the scroll which contains God's plan for enacting judgment and redemption upon the earth. Moreover, this will be testified to by the faithful witness of the people of God, a redeemed kingdom and priests, to the rule and presence of God in the world. The remaining chapters of the book of Revelation will flesh out in more detail how this will transpire.

REFLECTION

1. What do you think would be missing if chapters 4–5 were not in the book of Revelation?
2. How would you define worship based on these two chapters at the beginning of John's vision?
3. Some interpreters have concluded that John writes in symbols to hide the contents of the book, should

it fall into the wrong hands—Roman authorities. Do you think that what is going on in chapters 4–5 would have escaped the notice of the Roman government had they read it?

5

VISIONS OF JUDGMENT AND SALVATION I (REVELATION 6-16)

THE SEAL JUDGMENTS (CH. 6)

Chapter 6 records the opening of the first six of the seven seals on the scroll from chapter 5. In that chapter John recorded his vision of the Lamb who was worthy to take the scroll, because of his sacrificial death, and to unseal it and reveal its contents. Now in chapter 6 we find that scroll beginning to be unsealed, and as each seal is opened, a judgment takes place (except for seal 5). The fact that the judgments correspond to the seals before the scroll is actually opened probably suggests they are preliminary judgments. The entirety of the seal judgments, then, are to be seen as issuing from the throne in chapters 4–5, and are under the sovereign control of God and the

Lamb. The fact that there are seven seals indicates the completeness of God's judgment on the world. The point is not a historical sequence of seven judgments, but the fullness and completeness of God's initial judgments on the earth. The seals likely represent judgments beginning in the first-century hearers' own day living in the Roman Empire, and continuing until the sixth seal, the end-time Day of the Lord. The focus shifts from heaven in chapters 4–5 back to earth in chapter 6. The opening of the seventh seal is delayed until 8:1. The opening of the first six seals in this chapter also reveal a 4 + 2 pattern. The first four seals belong together as plagues that transpire on earth, having a close relationship to each other logically, conceptually, and structurally, revolving around the image of four horses and their riders. John narrates them all rather briefly. The fifth and sixth seals have a character of their own and are much longer in length of narration, with the fifth seal narrating the cry of the souls under the altar and the sixth seal bringing us to the events surrounding the final Day of the Lord at the end of history.

The First Four Seals (6:1–8)

In 6:1 the Lamb who took the scroll in chapter 5 begins to open the scroll by first unleashing its seals. That is, the Lamb will now initiate the process of bringing God's plan for judgment and salvation to earth. Appropriately, the four living creatures, under the authority of the Lamb, unleash the four seals upon the earth. The *four* living creatures symbolized the entirety of creation, and now the *four* seals represent the earthly judgments enacted by the Lamb opening the seals. The first four seals correspond to four horses and their riders, whose colors indicates their significance. The image of the horses is drawn from Zechariah 6:1–8. In Zechariah's vision, God commissions four groups of colored horses to patrol the earth and to bring judgment on the oppressors of God's people. Here in Revelation 6:1–8 the horses function in a similar manner, to bring judgment on those who persecute and oppress God's people.

When the first seal is opened (v. 1), one of the elders summons a rider on a white horse who rides out across the earth. The fact that the rider has a bow and a crown says something about the significance of this horse and its rider: they portray warfare and conquest. Though some take this as a positive image, referring to Jesus Christ who rides a white horse into battle in 19:11, the fact that the other three horses and their riders are negative images suggests that this one is as well. Perhaps it is to be seen as a parody or imitation of Christ and the victory he has accomplished (ch. 5).[1] The horse and its rider stand for warfare and conquest, probably reflecting the war and conquest by the Roman Empire in its expansion of its rule. Rome is bent on conquest in order to expand and maintain its empire. The remaining three seals and the horses (and horsemen) seem to unpack the meaning of the first one in more detail.

The second horse summoned by one of the four living creatures is fiery red in color (vv. 3–4). The color red symbolizes bloodshed. Three features of John's description of the rider reveal the significance of this horse and its color: it was able to take peace from the earth, cause people to kill one another, and it wielded a sword. This horse and its rider stand for internal conflict and fighting that takes place because of the Roman government's thirst for conquest in the first seal. In their desire for military conquest and expansion, the result would be internal strife, murder,

1. Beale, *Revelation*, 377.

and the loss of peace. In this sense, this second seal is an undermining of the Roman claim of establishing *Pax Romana* (Roman Peace). Its thirst for conquest paradoxically removes peace from within its borders in exchange for conflict and even death.

The third horse John sees is black in color (vv. 5–6). What the rider holds in his hand reveals something about what the horse and rider symbolize; the rider holds a scale, suggesting economic disparity. The voice indicates this disparity: an abundance of wine and olive oil, while bread was exorbitantly priced. This probably reflects the practice of Rome relying on the provinces to supply them wine and olive oil, luxuries that were unnecessary for sustaining life. But production of wine and olive oil to satisfy Rome left little room for growing the grain necessary for sustaining life. Particularly in times of famine, wheat and barley were out of reach of the average citizen. John sees an economy that is disordered, geared towards the Roman satisfaction of its own desires.

The fourth and final horse is pale green in color, and John tells us it symbolizes death (vv. 7–8). This seal is probably the culmination of the other three. The result of strife, conflict, warfare, famine, and unjust economic practices is death of those within the empire. Altogether, the four seals are God's judgment on the Roman rule and economy.[2] God's judgment consists of allowing Rome to reap the consequences of its thirst for power and conquest, and its economic practices and desire for its own comfort and prosperity.

---

2. Schüssler Fiorenza, *Revelation: Vision of a Just World*, 63.

Visions of Judgment and Salvation I (Revelation 6–16)

The Fifth and Sixth Seals (6:9–17)

The fifth seal (vv. 9-11) shifts back to heaven and contains a vision of the souls of the saints under the alter in heaven who have been martyred. Their cry, "How long, O Lord," is a cry for vindication from those who have put them to death for their witness and who have not yet seen justice. The response is to give them a white robe and tell them that there are more of their brothers and sisters that still have to be put to death for their faith. They are to be patient in waiting for their vindication. In a sense, the rest of the Revelation's vision through chapter 22 can be seen as an answer to their cry for vindication.[3] The sixth seal (vv. 12-17) shifts the focus back to earth and takes the reader to the brink of the end, the final Day of the Lord, and is an initial answer to the martyred saints' cry for vindication. The language of the breakup of the constellations comes from Old Testament texts (e.g. Isa 13:10; 34:4; Joel 2:10, 31; 3:15) and refers to the cosmic upheavals, symbolic of the effects of the coming of Christ in judgment at the end of history. The response of people to the Christ's coming in judgment is to prefer death by being crushed by falling rocks rather than face the wrath of the Lamb. This image also comes from Isaiah 2:10, 19, 21. The account ends with a question: "The great day of their wrath has come, and who is able to stand?" Chapter 7 will answer this question.

INTERLUDE: THE SEALING OF GOD'S PEOPLE AND THEIR FUTURE REWARD (CH. 7)

The answer to the question in 6:17, Who is able to stand in the Day of the Lord? is provided in chapter 7 with the vision of the people of God being protected by sealing (vv.

3. Leithart, *Revelation 1-11*, 309.

1–8), and then "standing" victorious before the Lamb (vv. 9–17). Chapter 7 is an interlude between the sixth and seventh seals that describes the relationship of the people of God to the seal judgments. The people of God are able to "stand" because they are protected from God's wrath by being sealed. The scene begins with four angels holding back the four winds of the earth. This symbolizes the holding back of judgment, with the four winds perhaps corresponding to the first four horses of chapter 6. The reason for this is stated in v. 3: until the servants of God are sealed, protecting them from God's judgment. Those who are sealed are identified as 144,000 taken from the twelve tribes of Israel, with 12,000 being sealed from each tribe. The 144,000 probably represent the church, the new people of God, consisting of Jews and Gentiles. The list of tribes does not correspond to any Old Testament list. It begins with the tribe of Judah, and Christ the Lamb has already been identified as from the tribe of Judah in 5:5. The twelve tribes are to be understood based on their relationship to Christ the Lamb. The 144,000 is based on 12 x 12, the number of the people of God squared (144), multiplied by 1000, a number of great magnitude.[4] The 144,000 symbolizes the complete people of God belonging to Jesus Christ. The counting of the tribes goes back to the Old Testament notion of a census of the people of Israel to determine their military strength (Num 2).[5] In other words, this scene of counting the twelve tribes suggests that the church is an army that goes out to do battle, yet paradoxically Revelation is clear that they conquer not with weapons of warfare but in the same way the Lamb did: through their suffering, faithful witness, even to death.

4. Ngunda, "Revelation," 1585.
5. Bauckham, *Climax of Prophecy*, 215–29.

Visions of Judgment and Salvation I (Revelation 6–16)

The next scene shifts to heaven and presents an innumerable, transcultural multitude of God's people standing victorious before the Lamb (vv. 9–17). This is a proleptic scene anticipating the fuller vision of final, eschatological salvation in 21:1—22:5. This multitude is likely the same group as the 144,000 since here we see the same "hear"/"see" pattern from chapter 5, where the same person, Jesus, was a Lion and a Lamb (John heard there was a lion, but saw a Lamb). Now in chapter 7 John "hears" the number 144,000, but what he "sees" is an innumerable multitude. John's images do not contradict each other but envision the same group from two different perspectives: as a mighty army, and as a victorious, numberless multitude, the numberless multitude probably reflecting the promises to Abraham of innumerable descendants (Gen 15:5; 22:17–18). Together, the images portray the church both as an army that conquers through their faithful witness, and now as standing victorious in the presence of the Lamb. As with the heavenly scene in chapters 4–5, they respond in worship to God and the Lamb because they have accomplished salvation for their people. The angelic world also joins in the worship (v. 11). In the rest of the scene is one of the rare instances of part of John's vision actually being explained for him. One of the elders raises the question of the identity of this multitude, and then answers John by identifying them as those who have survived the great tribulation, the entire time of the church's existence and struggle, and now stand in robes white from the blood of Christ; they have chosen to follow the slain Lamb. These may also be the "completed number" of martyrs from 6:11.

Further describing the scene (7:15–17), the elder uses images from the Old Testament that "flash forward" to the final vision in 21:1—22:5. The people of God serve as priests in God's tabernacling presence (21:3; 22:3–5; see Ezek 37:27). The people will never again experience physical hardship or sorrow in the new creation (21:4; see Isa 49:10; 25:8). And the Lamb will lead his people to springs of water (21:6; 22:1; see Isa 49:10). Therefore, those who are able to stand in the Day of the Lord are the people of God who are protected from God's wrath, who as a mighty army conquer by their faithful witness in the face of tribulation, and who will one day stand victorious in the presence of God and the Lamb and enjoy the reward of salvation. In contrast to those who hide from the face of God and the Lamb (6:16), the people of God now stand victorious in their presence.

THE SEVENTH SEAL AND THE SEVEN TRUMPET JUDGMENTS (CHS. 8–9)

After an intervening vision of the victorious people of God who will stand in the day of judgment (ch. 7), the sequence of seven seals, which was cut off after chapter 6, is resumed in chapter 8 as the seventh seal is finally opened (8:1). When the seventh seal is opened nothing happens; John says there is only silence. The reason for silence is probably explained in the next verses: so the prayers of the saints, which go up with the smoke of incense before God, can be heard (8:4). This suggests that the trumpet judgments are to be seen as a response to the prayers of the saints for vindication and justice (6:9–11). The silence also provides literary relief in the midst of the intense judgment scenes and are also a preparation for God's judgments to come. The peals of thunder and flashes of lightning anticipate judgment, and recall 4:5, suggesting that the trumpet judgments also issue from the throne.

Visions of Judgment and Salvation I (Revelation 6–16)

The first six trumpet judgments, like the seal judgments in chapter 6, reveal a 4 + 2 pattern, with the first four belonging together, and the last two being longer and of a different character. Trumpets five and six are also two of the three woes pronounced by an eagle in 8:13, setting them off from the first four trumpets. Further, like the seal judgments, the seventh trumpet is delayed until later (11:15–19), and there is intervening material (10:1—11:14). The precise relationship of the trumpets to the seals is unclear. The fact that the trumpet judgments are recorded after the seals does not mean that they take place chronologically after the seals have transpired. John's visions are recorded in the order in which he saw them, not necessarily the order in which they will actually take place. The trumpets are a more intense form of judgment than the seals, since unlike the seals that affected one-fourth of the earth, the trumpets now affect one-third. Most likely the reader is to see some overlap with the seals, but also a progression and intensification of God's judgment beyond the seals.

The trumpet judgments are clearly modeled after the Exodus plagues upon Egypt: hail (8:7), water turned to blood (8:8; see vv. 10–11), the sun darkened (8:12), and the locust plague (9:1–11). These parallel some of the plagues in Exodus 7–12. Like the first four seals, the first four trumpets unleash judgments upon the world and form a unit, the number four symbolizing the earth. Unlike the seals, the trumpets do not just affect the earth, but the sky and the seas also. It is difficult to determine exactly what these trumpet plagues symbolize, perhaps both spiritual and physical judgments. For example, the loss of ships in 8:9 may suggest economic loss.[6] More important than

---

6. Koester, *Revelation and the End of All Things*, 101.

deciphering each trumpet is to get a feel for the whole, the widespread devastation of God's judgment on wicked humanity, and what this section says about the nature of God's judgment. The main theological point of John's language is the certainty of God's judgment and to recall the Exodus. In the same way that God judged an evil, godless, and oppressive empire in the days of Egypt, so God will once again judge a wicked, godless, and oppressive empire in the form of Rome. And like the Egyptian plagues, God's people in Revelation are protected from God's judgment. Furthermore, these judgments, the bowls to follow in chapters 15–16, as well as the final judgments in chapters 19–20, emphasize a "de-creation" theme. That is, creation is being deconstructed or undone in judgment in order to make way for a new creation (21:1).

The last two trumpets take on a different character. The fifth trumpet is the first of three woes announced in 8:13. The fifth trumpet in 9:1–11 unleashes a swarm of locusts, again reflecting one of the Exodus plagues (Exod 10:1–20). The locusts emerge from the abyss in the midst of smoke. The abyss was the home of the demon world (see 11:7), which means that the locusts symbolize demonic beings as God's judgment on wicked humanity. John's description of them represents a grotesque combination of various animal, insect-like, and human features (vv. 7–8). The reference to the fact that they could torment humanity for five months represents the typical life cycle of a locust and points to the limitation of their threat, no matter how awful. Their leader is Abbadon or Apollyon, the latter term from the Greek word for "destroyer," but perhaps also a play on the name Apollos, a Roman god.[7] This bizarre description of the locusts is meant to 1) point to the horrific

---

7. Aune, *Revelation 6–16*, 535.

nature of God's judgment on humanity; and 2) contrast with the vision of heaven in chapters 4–5, where heaven is a place of order and symmetry. The four living creatures each had their own distinct face and form, whereas the locusts are now a grotesque chaotic combination of different animal and human parts. This points to the horrific situation of the world under judgment, under the rule of Satan the dragon and his demonic beings.[8]

The sixth trumpet, the second woe from 8:13, unleashes yet another hoard, an enormous cavalry (9:13–19). Once more, the scene is meant to be repulsive and evoke horror. The fact that smoke and sulfur come out of the mouths of the horses suggests that they also represent demonic beings. Yet, unlike the locusts who only harm humanity, during which time death will elude them (v. 6), the horses are able to kill humanity (v. 18). Like the Egyptian plagues where Pharaoh did not repent, humanity's response to the trumpet plagues is also a refusal to repent (vv. 20–22). Thus, the last two plagues are meant to show the horrific nature of God's judgment in the form of demonic powers unleashed against unrepentant humanity. The rhetorical function of this vision is to call the churches in chapters 2–3 to repent, as John has warned them to do.

INTERLUDE: THE LITTLE SCROLL AND THE TWO WITNESSES (CHS. 10–11)

The seventh trumpet is delayed. Intervening is a unified account of John receiving a scroll and being commissioned to prophesy (ch. 10), followed by a story of two witnesses (ch. 11), before the seventh trumpet finally is sounded (11:15–19). Usually commentaries refer to this

8. Koester, *Revelation and the End of All Things*, 102.

section, like chapter 7, as an "interlude." At one level, it functions to slow the action down of the series of trumpet judgments, delaying the seventh trumpet. Primarily, it addresses the question of the church's relationship to the trumpet plague judgments. In the same way the "interlude" in chapter 7 provided a commentary on the church's relationship to the seal judgments, so chapters 10–11 comment on the church's relationship to the trumpet judgments. These chapters will explain the cause of the church's persecution by the world and the basis for the plague judgments. The church, as a kingdom of priests, is to witness to the reality of God's kingdom here on earth. This will result in judgment upon their enemies. Most likely, the content of the scroll that John receives in chapter 10 is found in 11:1–13. In turn, chapter 11 foreshadows the content of the rest of 12:1—22:5.

John's Commission to Prophesy to the Nations (Ch. 10)

In Revelation 10 a colossal, Christ-like (see 1:9–16) angelic figure appears to John holding a scroll. The scroll is most likely the same scroll from chapter 5. There the scroll was sealed, but here it is given to John opened (v. 8) since its seals have been removed (ch. 6; 8:1–3). Now that the scroll has been opened, John is recommissioned to prophesy. The scene revolves around the speech of the angel to John. First, the angel commands John not to record the voices of the seven thunders (v. 4). When the angel cries out, seven thunders speak. The seven thunders probably symbolize seven further judgments that would follow the seals and trumpets (chs. 6; 8–9), but they are interrupted and John is told to seal up their contents and not write them down, so that they are not revealed. The reason for sealing up the seven thunders is because there is to be no more delay according

Visions of Judgment and Salvation I (Revelation 6–16)

to v. 6. At this point one might expect a further series of partial warning judgments: the seals affected one-fourth, the trumpets one-third, now we would expect a series of plagues that affect one-half. Yet now things will move quickly to the end, and the next series of plagues, the bowls (ch. 16), will be the final judgments and have no limitation. There will be no more warning judgments, but only the end narrated in chs. 16–22. Second, the angel takes an oath and proclaims that there will no longer be any delay (v. 6), but that God's purposes for judgment and salvation will be completed with the sounding of the seventh trumpet (in ch. 11). Even though there will still be several chapters left to go, the remaining chapters will unpack the seventh trumpet. This section functions to encourage the church in its faithful witness in the face of suffering.

The last three commands of the angel to John have to do with the scroll (vv. 8–11). First, John is commanded to take the scroll, probably the sealed scroll from chapter 5 that is now open. Second, he is to eat it, with the result that it will be sweet to his taste, but sour or bitter in his stomach, which imagery comes from Ezekiel 2:8—3:3. This suggests that its contents are about the fulfillment of God's promises (sweet), yet they carry a message of suffering and judgment (bitter). The final word of the angel to John is to prophesy again to the nations. This is probably to be seen as primarily a message of judgment, consistent with the bitter taste in John's mouth.

The Ministry of the Two Witnesses and the Seventh Trumpet (Ch. 11)

In Revelation 11 John begins to divulge the content of the open scroll from chapter 10. His message consists of two parts. First is the measuring of the temple in vv. 1–2.

John is given a measuring reed to measure the temple, drawing on Ezekiel 40–48. The temple is to be understood as metaphorical for the people of God themselves, not a literal building. The New Jerusalem/temple in Revelation 21:1—22:5 also draws on Ezekiel 40–48 and refers to the perfected people of God. Here, the temple refers to the earthly people of God. The act of measuring implies preservation and protection. However, only the main temple is measured, while the outer court is not measured and is given over to the Gentiles. This is meant to look at the church from two different perspectives: on the one hand, it is protected and preserved spiritually, while on the other hand, it will be persecuted and suffer outward, physical harm by the nations.[9] The time of the church's suffering is designated as forty-two months (11:2). In v. 3 the period of time of the two witnesses is 1260 days. These two references refer to the same period of time, and indicate an intense but limited period of time where the church is persecuted and tested. The rest of the chapter (vv. 3–12) will refer to the same reality and time period as the measured temple—the protected, yet persecuted church—but through the lens of a different image: two witnesses. The two witnesses, modeled after the Old Testament figures of Moses and Elijah, symbolize the entire witnessing church. The fact that there are two may reflect the fact that only two of the churches in chapters 2–3 are faithful (the others receive primarily censure). The time of their witness is forty-two months, symbolizing a short but intense time of testing. Their dress consisting of sackcloth indicates that they preach a message of repentance but that their message will result in judgment of the world who rejects them.[10]

9. Mounce, *Revelation*, 220.
10. Beale, *Revelation*, 576.

Visions of Judgment and Salvation I (Revelation 6–16)

The two witnesses metaphorically refer to the entire church, since the two witnesses are identified as the lampstands, which Jesus interpreted as the church in 1:20. On the one hand, the church symbolized by the two witnesses is protected (vv. 3–6). They carry out their witness without being harmed, and in fact are able to bring judgment plagues upon those who would attempt to harm them. The plagues they bring upon humanity likely refer to the plagues in chs. 8–9, explaining their basis: they come upon those who reject the witness of the church. On the other hand, the church suffers persecution and apparent defeat (vv. 7–10), similar to the fate suffered by Christ (they lie dead for three and one-half days). The beast comes out of the abyss and puts them to death, and their bodies lie in the street to be mocked by the world. John does not identify the beast here, having more to say in chapter 13. But the beast probably represented in John's day the Roman Empire. The "great city" here in all likelihood is a reference to Rome (see 17:18; 18:10, 16, 18, 19, 22).[11] John does not intend for this sequence of events to be taken temporally, as if the church will be successful in their witness for a time, and then towards the end of history they will be subject to persecution. Like the temple image in vv. 1–2, the experience of the two witnesses looks at the witnessing church from two perspectives, both of which will characterize its entire existence: it is protected spiritually and has success in its witness, yet at the same time it is persecuted physically and suffers apparent defeat. John, however, sees the two witnesses being resurrected and taken to heaven, which shows that the church, despite its apparent defeat, will be vindicated by God at the end of history, indicating that their witness and suffering was not in vain (vv. 11–13).

11. Trafton, *Reading Revelation*, 110.

Vindication is complete in v. 13 with God's judgment, and people respond with terror and giving glory to God. Verse 14 concludes the interlude in 10:1—11:13. It announces that two of the three woes anticipated back in 8:13 have already passed. These two woes are to be associated with the fifth and sixth trumpet judgments of chapter 9. The reader can anticipate that the third woe is coming soon. The fact that the first two woes correspond to the fifth and sixth trumpets might suggest that the third woe corresponds to the seventh trumpet coming next. However, it is more likely that the third woe refers to 12:12, where a "woe" is pronounced on the earth with the defeat and casting down of the dragon to earth to wreak havoc.[12]

The seventh trumpet is finally sounded in 11:15–18, which the angel in 10:6–7 said would happen without delay when sounded. The content of the seventh trumpet is found in two speeches. The first is from unidentified loud voices that proclaim that the transfer of the dominion of this world to the dominion of Jesus Christ has now taken place, a dominion that will last forever (v. 15). The second, in response, is the twenty-four elders who worship and proclaim the Lord God has established his reign. This involves both judgment of the wicked and rewarding the faithful people of God (vv. 16–18). The rest of the book will reveal how God will bring about final judgment (chs. 19–20) and reward his people (20:4–6; 21:1—22:5). In response to the voices in vv. 15–18, heaven is opened in v. 19 so that God's judgments can take place in fulfillment of God's promises.

---

12. For this view see Resseguie, *Revelation*, 167; Paul, *Revelation*, 206.

Visions of Judgment and Salvation I (Revelation 6–16)

THE DRAGON, CHILD, WOMAN, AND TWO BEASTS: THE CHURCH IN COSMIC CONFLICT (CHS. 12–13)

Revelation 12–22 will now further develop the themes that are introduced in chapter 11, especially the seventh trumpet from 11:15–18. One of the themes from chapter 11 was the war on the people of God by the beast that comes up out of the abyss (11:7). Before developing the themes of God's reign, his judgment, and his rewarding of the saints, John explores in more detail the source of the persecution of God's people by the beast in chapters 12–13 as the basis for God's judgment of their enemies. These chapters are also linked to chapter 11 by the same reference to the duration of the church's activity and persecution (11:2, 3; see 12:6, 14; 13:5). In this section John unveils the true nature of the church's conflict by showing the supernatural forces behind their earthly struggle. The main characters are the woman, the dragon, the son, the woman's offspring, and two beasts.

The Woman, the Dragon, and the Son (Ch. 12)

The vision begins with a woman in heavenly attire (v. 1). She probably represents the entirety of the people of God, both in the Old Testament and New Testament, since she plays a role before and after the birth of the son, a reference to Christ. She is pregnant with a son, and the dragon pursues her in order to kill her son as soon as it is born. The son is clearly Jesus, the Messiah, as indicated by the reference to Psalm 2:9 in v. 5. John's story also reflects stories in the Greco-Roman world of dragon or serpent-like figures who pursue a woman who is about to give birth to a son, usually a god, and the son is hidden and protected from the serpent. The son here in Revelation 12 is taken up to heaven, a reference to Jesus' ascension (and resurrection?) before the dragon can get to him, and the woman symbolizing the church is taken to the desert, a place of preservation and safety. The time she is there, 1260 days (v. 6), corresponds to the same period of time the temple and the witnesses are subject to suffering and persecution (11:2, 3). These three images, the measuring of the temple, the success of the witnesses, and the preservation of the woman, all communicate the same idea: the church will ultimately be protected spiritually, even though it may suffer harm physically in the form of persecution.

There are two other scenes found in chapter 12. First is a battle between the dragon, who is identified as Satan and the serpent from Genesis 3, and Michael the archangel in heaven. This scene further interprets the story of the woman, dragon, and son in vv. 1–6. Satan is defeated and cast to earth. Verse 11 provides the clue as to when this battle and expulsion from heaven takes place: it is a result of the death of Christ. The defeat of Satan and being cast to earth becomes the occasion for a heavenly voice in response (vv. 10–12), which interprets the significance of the defeat of Satan. On the one hand, with Satan's defeat the rule and authority of Christ has replaced the dominion and authority of Satan over this world. On the other hand, though defeated, Satan still wreaks havoc on the earth because he knows his time is short. The saints can only overcome in the same way the dragon was defeated—by the blood of Christ and their faithful testimony, even to the point of death.

In the second scene, Satan goes after the woman, who is protected in the desert for three-and-one-half years (vv. 13–16). This period of time, once more, corresponds

Visions of Judgment and Salvation I (Revelation 6–16)

to the 1260 days and the forty-two months of the temple's and the witnesses' persecution (ch. 11). Frustrated from being unable to attack the woman, the dragon goes after and persecutes her offspring (v. 17), who are identified as those who obey God's commands and who keep their faithful witness to Jesus, the church. The woman and her offspring both symbolize the same thing, the people of God, but like the temple and the two witnesses, from two different perspectives: the people of God are kept safe spiritually (the woman), but are subject to physical harm in the form of persecution (her offspring). The entire chapter demonstrates that behind the church's earthly struggle and persecution at the hands of earthly authorities (ch. 11) lies the hostility of Satan to Jesus Christ and to his people. By identifying the dragon as Satan and serpent (v. 9), the enmity between the serpent and the woman, and her offspring, John connects this story with Genesis 3:15 ("And I will put enmity between you and the woman, and between your offspring and hers"), to show that the conflict the church faces is nothing less than the age-old conflict that goes all the way back to the creation narrative.

The Two Beasts Who Assist the Dragon (Ch. 13)

In Revelation 13 John introduces us to two beastly figures. The events in chapter 13 do not take place chronologically after chapter 12, but explore in more detail how the dragon carries out his persecuting activity from chapter 12—through the aid of two dragon-like beasts. That chapter 13 refers to the same events as chapter 12 can be seen by the fact that John says the first beast carries out its work for a period of forty-two months (13:5), the same time as the dragon's persecution of the people of God in 12:6, 14. The first beast is described as similar to the dragon, since he represents him (13:1–10). A beast-like figure would have meant chaos, evil, and oppression, and the sea from which it comes suggests its evil origin. Most likely the beast symbolizes the Roman Empire and/or the emperor. By portraying him as a beast, John reveals the true source of Rome's hostility toward Christians. This beast is a composite of the four beasts from Daniel's vision (Dan 7:4–8); now Rome is the culmination of all the evil empires of the past. It also has a head that appeared to survive a death blow (v. 3). Though this might have a specific historical referent (the myth of Nero coming back to life), it primarily points to the apparent invincibility of the empire and is a satanic parody of the Lamb who was slain (5:6) and yet lives.[13] Verses 3–4 describe the beast's activity in relationship to the world. The first beast's primary responsibility in the narrative is to exercise authority over the earth on behalf of the dragon (v. 2). He receives the worship of the entire earth (in contrast to the worship that is given to God and the Lamb in heaven in chapters 4–5) and he directs worship towards the dragon. Verses 5–10 describe the beast's relationship to the people of God. He blasphemes their God and wages war against them. Those belonging to the Lamb are persecuted by the beast and are called to endurance and faithful witness (vv. 7–10).

The second beast (vv. 11–18) is described as coming from the land and probably symbolizes the local authorities in Asia minor that are responsible for promoting the imperial cult and allegiance to Rome. Later in Revelation this beast is called the "false prophet" (16:13; 19:20; 20:10) because he deceived people into worshiping the dragon rather than Christ. The beast looks like a lamb, thoroughly

---

13. Mounce, *Revelation*, 253.

deceptive and a false savior.[14] The events in these verses do not happen following the activity of the first beast, but further describe how the first beast carries out his persecuting activity on the church. Therefore, John sets up a chain of authority: Dragon → Beast #1 → Beast #2

The responsibility of the second beast is to promote worship of the first beast (Rome and its emperor), probably through promoting emperor worship in Asia Minor. He does this primarily through deception. The setting up of an image and breathing life into it probably is not meant to refer to any specific historical practice, but symbolizes the deceptive nature of imperial practice and its effect. The other way that the second beast exercises its authority throughout the empire on behalf of the first beast is by imposing economic sanctions (vv. 16–18). The second beast will force people to receive a mark on their hand or forehead, the mark symbolizing allegiance to Imperial Rome and the system of emperor worship. It contrasts with the mark that the saints receive on their forehead in 7:3, which indicates their allegiance to God and the Lamb. Economic and commercial activity would have been tied closely to religious practice and the imperial cult. A refusal to participate in the imperial system of worship would have economic consequences: Christians would be unable to participate in everyday economic transactions.[15] The mark is further identified as the number of the beast which is 666. Though the precise significance of this number may be lost to the modern reader, it is likely that the number reflects the numerical value of the name of the emperor Nero, a process known as *gematria* (adding up the numerical values of the letters of a name). By identifying the

14. Ngundu, "Revelation," 1592.
15. Mounce, *Revelation*, 263.

number with Nero's name, John is not claiming that Nero is the current emperor, but given Nero's evil character as a tyrant of all tyrants, the image says something about the true nature of the Empire and its current emperor. It is also possible that 666 is to be seen as falling short of the perfect number 777, suggesting further its association with evil and anti-godly powers. Thus, John is telling his readers that taking on the mark of the beast is to associate with the anti-godly powers of evil. It would be better for them to suffer the economic sanctions. Overall, chapters 12–13 explore the true source of the church's conflict with Rome. John unmasks the true nature of their struggle; behind it ultimately lies Satan and the chaotic powers of evil at work to oppose God's kingdom and his people. However, Satan has already been defeated, and while the church is subject to physical harm and persecution, it is preserved spiritually. This is why the church's enemies will be judged. John's reader should endure in their resistance and faithful witness, no matter what the consequences.

VISIONS OF JUDGMENT AND SALVATION (CH. 14)

Chapter 14 narrates the outcome of the conflict in chapters 12–13, with visions of judgment of those who follow the beast, and salvation for the faithful persecuted. The reference to the seal or mark (or name) written on forehead or hand (vv. 1, 9, 11) and worshiping the beast and his image clearly links chapter 14 back to chapter 13. This chapter begins with a contrasting scene to chapters 12–13 with the saints, who were subject to the dragon and beast's persecuting activity and who refused their mark, now standing victorious on Mt. Zion with the Father's name on their forehead. They are identified as the 144,000 from chapter 7. That is, the saints are depicted as a victorious army who have conquered through their faithful witness. Now they stand victorious before God, and they are morally pure (v. 5). The image of them as males abstaining from sexual intercourse does not suggest the people are only male, but is a symbol consistent with the Old Testament requirement of abstaining from sexual relations for engaging in holy war (see Deut 20; 23:9-10; 1 Sam 21:5; 2 Sam 11:11), here referring to their spiritual purity and loyalty.[16] John hears a sound that first is like cascading water and loud thunder, but then turns out to be the sound of harps (v. 2). They introduce the song that the saints sing, though the words are not recorded.

Then there follows a contrasting section that turns to God's judgment on those who have followed the beast from chapter 13 (vv. 6-13). It is structured around the proclamation of three angels. The first angel calls for repentance in light of God's judgment. The second angel announces the fall of Babylon, a cipher for Rome, because of her immorality, and making other nations complicit in her immorality. The fall of Babylon/Rome will get narrated more fully in chapter 18. The third angel proclaims judgment on all those who worshiped the beast from chapter 13 and who took his mark. By contrast, in an editorial remark (v. 12) on this part of the vision, John calls on the saints to endure and continue to obey God's commands because God's judgment is coming on those who follow the beast. The final section of chapter 14 consists of two scenes: the harvest of the earth (vv. 14-16) and the harvest of grapes (vv. 17-20). Though the two images could refer to parallel images of judgment, more likely they refer to contrasting

---

16. Witherington, *Revelation*, 185-86.

images of salvation and judgment.[17] The first image of the Son of Man harvesting the earth refers to the salvation of the saints. The image of the harvest of the grapes, then, refers to the judgment of the ungodly, since there is mention of the winepress of the wrath of God. The image of harvest and treading grapes in a wine press was a symbol of judgment in the Old Testament (Isa 63:3; Joel 3:13), and the image of blood up to the horses' bridals comes from apocalyptic texts (1 Enoch 100:3). So these two final harvest scenes reinforce the vision of salvation that is in store for the faithful people of God, and the judgment in store for those who follow the beast.

THE LAST JUDGMENT SERIES: THE SEVEN BOWLS (CHS. 15-16)

These two chapters narrate the final series of seven-fold judgments. The fact that the effect of the first two series consisting of seals (one-fourth) and trumpets (one-third) were only partial would lead the reader to expect a further series of partial, preliminary judgments (one-half). However, the bowl judgments contain no such limitation, and of them it is said that "with them God's wrath is completed" (15:1). As 10:5 proclaimed, there would be no more delay, but now only final judgment and salvation. This can also be seen in that there is no interlude between the sixth and seventh plagues, as there was with the seals and trumpets. Chapter 15 provides the introduction to the pouring out of the last plagues, introducing the seven angels who hold the seven bowls filled with the final outpouring of God's wrath (vv. 1, 5-8). This introduction to the bowls is "interrupted" by a vision of a sea of glass and those who

17. See Bauckham, *Climax of Prophecy*, 290-96.

Visions of Judgment and Salvation I (Revelation 6–16)

overcame the beast and his image standing by the sea and singing the song of Moses (vv. 3–4). This interruption, before the bowls are actually poured out, seems to function in three ways. First, it juxtaposes once more a contrasting vision of the salvation and reward of the saints with the judgment of their enemies. Second, it further develops the Exodus motif with the singing of the Song of Moses by the sea, as Moses and the Israelites did after their redemption from slavery in Egypt (Exod 15), following the plagues. The trumpet plagues, as we will see, are also modeled on the Exodus plagues. Third, the song makes it clear that the plagues are an expression of God's justice and truth, in order to draw the nations to himself.

The narration of the plagues themselves follows in chapter 16. These plagues are probably to be understood as God's final judgment at the very end of the age. The fact that they are identified as the completion of God's "wrath" links them with the mention of God's wrath in the endtime judgment in 14:19 (cf. also 6:16–17). The key point is not to figure out exactly what these judgments are and what they look like, but the theological point of the certainty and nature of God's judgment. It also resonates with the Exodus theme: just as certainly as God poured out his plagues on an evil, godless empire as a prelude to redeeming his people in Egypt, so he will do it once more. Hence, a number of the bowl plagues are modeled on the Exodus: sores on people (Bowl 1), water turned to blood (Bowls 2–3), darkness (Bowl 5), frogs (Bowl 6), and hail (Bowl 7) (see Exodus 7–11). Though the text concludes that with the seventh seal "it is done," there are still five more chapters to come. However, the last two bowls will get unpacked in much more detail in several of the following chapters. The sixth bowl narrates the gathering of the kings of the earth for the battle of Armageddon, though nothing beyond that happens here. The kings are only prepared for battle, leaving the reader waiting for the outcome. The seventh bowl refers briefly to the judgment on Babylon/Rome. These last two bowl judgments will receive further elaboration in the next few chapters in reverse order: a description of Babylon and its destruction in chapters 17–18, and the final battle in 19:11–21 (see also 20:7–10). Also, the "unholy trinity" will get disposed of in chapters 19–20 in the reverse order in which it was introduced in chapters 12–13.

REFLECTION

1. How does judgment play a role within God's overall plan to establish his kingdom and rule over all of creation? How would you summarize the purpose of God's judgment?

2. How would you describe the church's role in the establishment of God's kingdom on earth?

3. What is the relationship between the seals, trumpets, and bowls? Does it make sense to see them as completely overlapping? Or do they occur in succession (the seals, then the trumpets, then the bowls)? Or a combination of these two approaches?

6

VISIONS OF JUDGMENT AND SALVATION II (REVELATION 17-20)

This section of Revelation (chs. 17–20) constitutes a series of "removal" scenes, where God removes through judgment everything that stands in the way of the establishment of his kingdom on earth, in the form of a new heavens and new earth, for his people to enjoy. First, Babylon/Rome is judged (chs. 17–18), followed by the judgment of the two beasts from chapter 13 and all of rebellious humanity in a final battle (19:11–21). Then Satan is judged (20:1–10), and finally everything, including the present creation, is removed (20:11–15). As we saw with the trumpets and bowls, there is a "de-creation" through judgment, as the cosmos is being deconstructed and undone in order to make way for a new creative act (21:1—22:5).

THE FALL OF BABYLON (CHS. 17-18)

Revelation 17–18 expands the seventh seal (16:17–21) with a description of Babylon and her judgment and fall. John and his readers would have identified Babylon with first-century Rome, the city on seven hills (17:9). For those churches like Laodicea (3:14–22) who are compromising with Rome and its economic system, and for churches like Smyrna suffering for their allegiance to Christ rather than Rome (2:8–11), this vision shows Rome in its true colors and its ultimate destruction to encourage the latter church to stay the course, but the former to rethink their allegiance to Rome. Chapter 17 is primarily an account of what John *sees*, the prostitute Babylon. Chapter 18 is primarily an account of what John *hears*, the announcement of judgment on Babylon and the responses of various groups to her fall.

A Vision of the Prostitute-Babylon (Ch. 17)

In John's third "in the Spirit" experience (17:1; see 1:10; 4:2; 21:10) John sees a vision of a woman riding on a beast (v. 3), the same beast introduced in previous chapters (chs. 11; 13). This chapter can be divided into two sections: John's vision of the woman riding the beast (vv. 1–6), followed by the angel's interpretation of the vision for John (vv. 7–18). The woman John sees is identified as a prostitute (v. 1), an Old Testament image for seduction and unfaithfulness (Isa 23:14–18; Nah 3:1–4), and she wears the attire of a harlot (vv. 4–5). Perhaps John is overturning popular conceptions of Rome as goddess Roma. Instead of a goddess, Rome is a harlot and seductress. The fact that the woman rides on the beast with ten horns (from Dan 7:7) and seven heads shows that she is supported by the satanic power of evil and chaos. She is guilty of making

Visions of Judgment and Salvation II (Revelation 17–20)

the kings and nations drunk with her adulteries, an image of seducing the nations into entering into economic alliance with her and reliance on her. The image also suggests victimization.[1] She is portrayed as decked out in expensive clothes and jewels that she has acquired at the expense of those that she has exploited (v. 4). Furthermore, she is guilty of the blood of the people of God whom she has put to death (v. 6). Verse 5 identifies the woman as Babylon the Great, a "code" name for Rome. The picture is of Rome who is guilty of arrogant self-reliance and exploitation of others for her own wealthy desires, and also seducing the nations into reliance on her. She is also guilty of violence and murder of the people of God.

In response to John's astonishment at this vision (v. 6), an angel interprets features of the vision for John in vv. 7–18, showing that the woman's apparent beauty and allurement are only a façade for her true nature and identity. The features that will be the object of the angel's interpretation are the beast, its seven heads, the ten horns, and the water upon which the woman sits, and finally the woman. The exact identity of the beast is not revealed, but in light of chapter 13 it represents the power of Rome and its emperor. The fact that it comes out of the abyss suggests its demonic and evil nature. The angel identifies the beast in vv. 7–8 as the one "who was, is not, and is about to come up out of the abyss and go into destruction." This shows that the beast is a demonic parody of God "who was, and is, and is to come" (4:8). But the beast is no match for God, for when the beast "comes" he is going into destruction. The phrase may also recall common stories about Nero, that he had apparently died ("is not") but was rumored to be hiding and ready to return in the

---

1. Mathewson, "Social Justice in the Book of Revelation," 185–86.

future. Nevertheless, the point is that despite the claims and power of the beast (the beastly power of Rome), it is headed for destruction (judgment).

The angel then interprets the two other main features of the beast: his seven heads and his ten horns. The seven heads actually get a double interpretation (v. 9). First, the seven heads symbolize seven hills upon which the woman sits, clearly reflecting common ancient conceptions of Rome as the city on the seven hills.[2] Second, the seven heads also represent seven kings, probably Roman emperors. Despite attempts to identify seven specific historical emperors, it is probably better to understand the number seven as symbolic of the entire, complete rule of Rome and its emperors. As we have already seen, numbers are used symbolically throughout Revelation, and that is the case here. Further, John tells the reader that five have already fallen, there is one who now is, and another that is still to come (v. 10). There is also an eighth king, which is identified as the beast and seems to extend the rule of the seven (v. 11). What is the point of this description? It is mainly to show that, despite the seeming invincibility of Rome and its ability to continue even after the falling of several emperors, Rome's rule is not going to last forever. In fact, Roman rule has nearly run its course (five have already fallen, with only two more to go!), even though it appears to extend itself with an eighth. As Revelation indicates elsewhere, the coming of Christ to consummate the promised kingdom of God is soon (1:3; 22:7, 12, 20). This will mean the end of all worldly rulers. Because Christ is coming soon, the time of worldly rule is almost at its end. This is a direct affront to Rome's claim to be eternal (*Roma Aeterna*).

2. Koester, *Revelation*, 690.

Visions of Judgment and Salvation II (Revelation 17–20)

The next items that the angel interprets for John are the ten horns of the beast (vv. 12–14), which allude to Daniel 7:7. Once more, the number "ten" is a symbolic number, suggesting totality and completeness, rather than ten specific first-century kings. The ten horns are identified as ten additional kings different from the seven heads/kings. The ten horns then refer to the totality of kingdoms that collaborate with Rome and share their power with it ("with the beast," v. 12); they give power and authority to the beast (Rome and its emperors) (v. 13). The "one hour" of their rise to power points to the short, limited nature of their reign. This coalition of the beast and the totality of kings is no match for the Lamb, who will readily defeat them, bringing an end to their rule (v. 14).

The next feature of the vision that gets interpreted is the waters upon which the woman sits (vv. 15). The waters are identified by the angelic interpreter as "peoples, multitudes, nations, and tongues." The image of sitting suggests authority or control over, particularly through its seduction and economic exploitation. The next feature of the angel's interpretation is not explicitly found in the vision of vv. 1–6, but gives further details of the relationship between the beast, the ten horns, and the woman (vv. 16–18). In a surprising turn-about, John records that the beast and the ten kings, who were in coalition with the empire, will turn on the woman (Rome, see v. 18) and destroy her. Intriguingly, the beast is Rome and its emperor (see ch. 13), but also turns against and destroys the woman, who is Rome! The point seems to be that Roman rule and its coalition with the rulers of the world in their monopoly over the nations will self-destruct, pointing to the self-destructive nature of evil and thirst for power.[3]

---

3. Boxall, *Revelation*, 249.

That is, God allows the godless, violent nature of Roman power to come to its full expression in its self-destruction.[4] Verse 17 makes this clear by attributing Rome's self-destruction to divine providence: God has given the kings one heart in order to accomplish God's purpose. Then to remove any uncertainty, the woman that John saw is identified in v. 18 as the great city, Rome, who rules over the kings of the earth (apparently different than the ten kings). This introduction of the prostitute/Babylon/Rome and its detailed description, along with a brief mention of her downfall, forms the backdrop for chapter 18, which will focus on her destruction.

Responses to Babylon's Fall (Ch. 18)

In this chapter we encounter a section of a different literary character than the previous chapter. While chapter 17 was a vision with an accompanying interpretation, chapter 18 records the verbal responses of different groups surrounding Babylon's (Rome's) judgment.[5] John does not actually see the destruction of Babylon, but only sees different individuals or groups and hears their cries of mourning or rejoicing in response to Rome's judgment. Most of the language in the section is drawn from the Old Testament, particularly Ezekiel 26–28 and it oracles against Tyre, which is condemned for its idolatry, pride, and greed, and Isaiah 47:7–8 against Babylon. The first two responses to Babylon's fall in Revelation 18 come from heavenly voices (vv. 1–8). The first voice issues from an angel who descends from heaven (vv. 1–3). This angelic voice announces the downfall of Babylon ("Fallen, fallen is Babylon the great";

---

4. Paul, *Revelation*, 289.
5. Paul, *Revelation*, 289.

Visions of Judgment and Salvation II (Revelation 17–20)

Isa 21:9). The result of her judgment is that she will be a home for demons and all unclean things. Her judgment will leave her desolate and reveal her true demonic nature. The reason for her judgment is that once again she has caused the rulers of the earth to commit adultery, a metaphor for seducing them into engaging in her idolatrous, unjust economic practices (see 17:1–6). The second voice from heaven is anonymous (vv. 4–8). This heavenly voice begins with a call for God's people to leave Babylon (v. 4), which is not so much a call to come out physically, but a call to spiritually disassociate with her and refuse to participate in her idolatrous, godless practices and so compromise their faithfulness. This is urgent for the people of God in order to avoid the judgment that is coming upon her and all those complicit in her adulterous activities. The reason for her judgment is spelled out in vv. 5–7 utilizing Old Testament language. Her sins are so many that they have reached up to heaven to God. The image of God paying her back double, or mixing a double portion (v. 6) should not be taken to mean that Babylon will receive twice the amount of punishment that she doled out. Rather the idea is more accurately of "reduplication." What she gave out will be reduplicated in her judgment; that is, she will receive judgment equivalent to what she did (the punishment fits the crime).[6] The reason that she will be judged is that she has indulged in luxury, has pursued her own glory (and not God's), and arrogantly claimed self-sufficiency ("I am seated as a queen!" v. 7). For this reason her judgment at the hands of God will be swift and certain (v. 8).

The next "voice" that the reader hears in response to Babylon's fall is that of the kings of the earth who

---

6. See Beale, *Book of Revelation*, 901; Smalley, *Revelation to John*, 447–48.

committed adultery with her and shared in her luxury (vv. 9–10; cf. 17:3). They sing a funeral dirge ("Woe") to lament Rome's fall. Again, adultery is a metaphor for sharing in her (Rome's) unjust, idolatrous economic practices. The rulers of the earth mourn her downfall because it means the end of their benefitting off her economy. They have become wealthy by selling and trading with Rome.

The next group whose "voice" is heard in the form of another funeral dirge ("Woe") is the merchants who have benefitted from Rome's economy through selling to them (vv. 11–17). The extravagant nature of Rome's economic practices is illustrated further in the list of items in vv. 12–13. The list of cargo depicts the excessive luxury and extravagance of Rome. Furthermore, it may point to the exploitative nature of Rome's economy: these items flow into Rome at the expense of the rest of the world, even though some grow rich off trade with Rome.[7] The most unsettling item in the list is saved for last: slaves. They are treated as commodities to be traded and sold, but John adds that they are "human souls." Elaborating on the merchants' response from v. 11, their dirge for the prostitute/Babylon is found in vv. 16–17a: her wealth is now gone, the source of her beauty and the merchants' own gain.[8]

The next voice belongs to those who make a living off the sea (vv. 17b–19). Like the other two groups, they stand far off, observing the destruction of the great city. They mourn for the same reason: they benefitted from Rome's wealth and economy. Now it has been brought to ruins. The cries of woe in response to Rome's judgment would be an especially poignant message to those churches, such

---

7. Mathewson, "Social Justice in the Book of Revelation," 187–88.
8. Paul, *Revelation*, 299.

Visions of Judgment and Salvation II (Revelation 17–20)

as Laodicea, who are wealthy and who have compromised with Rome and its system.

The final voice in v. 20 is difficult to identify. It obviously cannot be the voice of those who work the sea in vv. 17–19, nor does it seem to be the mighty angel that is introduced in v. 21. Rather, it is likely the voice of the angel from 18:1–4, or possibly even John's own voice.[9] In contrast to the mourning of the various groups in the previous verses, the saints are called upon to rejoice because God's justice has been demonstrated in vindicating his people by visiting on Rome the same measure she has given to the saints, a further fulfillment of the cry of the saints for vindication back in 6:10.

The final "voice" in this section belongs to a mighty angel (vv. 21–24). The angel first performs a symbolic act of throwing a millstone into the sea to illustrate the powerful nature and the suddenness of the destruction of Babylon. The angel's speech then interprets the significance of Rome's judgment. John depicts it in terms of the absence of all those things that once made Rome a city bustling with activity and joyful sounds: no music or musicians, no workers and the sounds of their industry, no light, no joy at weddings, no activities of merchants. The reason for this is that Rome has seduced the nations into participating in its idolatrous, unjust economic practices. In a climactic statement (v. 24), it is guilty of the murder of Christians, but also others who live on the earth.[10] Therefore, chapter 18 begins and ends with the voice of an angel announcing Babylon's judgment. In between are three dirges by various groups who benefitted from Rome, lamenting her destruction. John interprets the significance of Babylon's

---

9. Paul, *Revelation*, 300.

10. Schüssler Fiorenza, *Revelation: Vision of a Just World*, 95.

judgment through this series of "voices" that respond to Babylon's fall. The judgment of the seventh bowl (16:19) where God remembers Babylon the Great is now fulfilled. Although Babylon/Rome appears glamorous and invincible, John unveils its true nature: it is corrupt, godless, evil, and guilty of murdering the saints and people on the earth. Therefore, it is destined for destruction, and God's people are called to disassociate with it.

THE WEDDING SUPPER OF THE LAMB (19:1–10)

Despite the chapter break, 19:1–10 belongs to the account of Babylon's fall narrated in chapters 17–18, in that it depicts the rejoicing of all heaven in response to Babylon-Rome's judgment (vv. 1–10). In stark contrast to the "voices" of lament in chapter 18, now there are "voices" of rejoicing at Babylon's fall. In contrast to the three "Woes" that dominated chapter 18, three times a group is depicted as shouting "Hallelujah," meaning "Praise the Lord" (19:1, 3, 4, 6). In vv. 1–3 a great heavenly multitude praises God because he has demonstrated his justice and saved his people by delivering them from the oppressive, evil power of the Roman Empire. The next group is the twenty-four elders and four living creatures (vv. 4–5) introduced in Revelation 4–5. They join the great multitude in shouting "Hallelujah" in response to God's judgment of Babylon. Then an unidentified voice from the throne calls on everyone to worship God because of his just judgments (v. 5). In response, a great multitude praises God because he has established his kingdom. With the judgment of Babylon and its rule, God's just reign has now been realized. Furthermore, alongside of the judgment of Babylon comes the vindication of the saints: Now they celebrate the wedding supper of the Lamb. The imagery of a wedding and a bride contrasts with the imagery of the prostitute and seduction in chapters 17–18. Nuptial imagery was used in the Old Testament to refer to Yahweh's relationship to Israel (Isa 54:1–8; Hos 1–3), and in the New Testament this imagery gets picked up to refer to Christ's relationship to his church (Eph 5:22–33). The future salvation of God's people is sometimes compared to the celebration of a wedding or to a banquet in the Old Testament (Isa 60–62; Isa 25:6–8; see Luke 22:18). Now the marriage between Christ and his people is consummated in the end-time banquet in Revelation 19:6–8. Furthermore, the white linen worn by the saints as wedding garments is identified as their good deeds, within the context of Revelation probably a reference to their allegiance, faithfulness, and endurance. The white linen contrasts with the gaudy, extravagant dress of the prostitute in 17:1–3. God's reign means judgment and mourning for those who relied on Babylon, but it means rejoicing and salvation for the people of God. The section concerning the judgment of Babylon ends with John's interaction with the angelic figure that has accompanied him on this vision (vv. 9–10). First, it directs true worship to God, not the angelic mediator. Second, true prophecy serves to testify to Jesus and to obedience to him.

THE FINAL BATTLE AND DEFEAT OF THE TWO BEASTS (19:11–21)

Following the vision of the judgment of the harlot-Babylon, the scene shifts in 19:11 to another judgment scene, which is depicted as a final battle (19:11–21). This battle is an expansion of the sixth bowl in 16:12–16, which contains the battle of Armageddon, though the sixth bowl only has the kings gathered for battle, but says nothing of the fighting or outcome, leaving the reader expecting further elaboration. Now that battle is finally narrated in detail here in 19:11–21. For the moment the wedding supper of the Lamb and the consummated wedding are delayed, since there are more judgments to take place before the bride is reintroduced in all her glory (ch. 21).[11] The scene begins with John once again seeing heaven opened (19:11). In the same way that John's vision began with an open heaven (4:1), John once more sees heaven opened to introduce the climactic judgment of God at the end of history (what theologians call Christ's second coming). What will follow is a series of visions that will narrate the result of heaven opened and Christ's end-time return to consummate God's plan of salvation. That is, chapters 19–20 are a series of snapshots that narrate the outcome of the return of Christ to earth at the end of history. They do not indicate a chronological progression, but are different perspectives on what happens when Christ returns at the end of history. A number of important observations will guide us in understanding this account of the end-time battle in 19:11–21.

1. The rider on the white horse is described in 19:11–16 with language drawn from the Old Testament and elsewhere in Revelation to show that Christ is a powerful warrior and judge who comes to render judgment. The emphasis is on the fact that he will judge justly and truly. With his eyes of fire he is able to see everything. The crown on his head signifies victory. The blood-stained garment in v. 13 may refer to the blood of Christ's enemies (see Isa 63:1–4), or it may refer to Christ's own blood shed on the cross through which he is victorious. That this is a reference to Christ is clear from his description as the

11. Koester, *Revelation and the End of All Things*, 168.

"Word of God" (see John 1:1) and the quotation of Psalm 2:9 ("He will rule them with an iron scepter"; see Rev 12:5). He is also the "King of Kings and Lord of Lords" (v. 16). Yet Christ also has a name that no one knows, indicating that he can be known, but he cannot be controlled or mastered (v. 12).[12]

2. Though a battle scene is depicted, conspicuously no fighting actually takes place. The armies of heaven (angels, or the 144,000, or both?) that accompany Christ into battle, in fact, do no fighting and seem unnecessary (v. 14). The enemies are simply destroyed by the sword coming out of the rider's mouth (vv. 19–21) in judgment.

3. This lack of actual fighting and the presence of the sword that comes out of the rider's mouth suggests the motif of a judgment scene (vv. 15, 21), symbolized by a battle, rather than referring to an actual battle. Judgment takes place by the word that comes from Christ's mouth.

4. All the nations and kings of the earth who oppose Christ are judged, but the focus is on the judgment of the two beasts who were introduced in chapter 13 as the antagonists of God and persecutors of the church. They are the ones who now are responsible for gathering the armies and leading them into battle (the account of the dragon being judged in the same battle will come later in chapter 20).

5. The grisly feast announced in vv. 17–18, where the birds feast on the dead bodies, contrasts with the glorious wedding supper of the Lamb in 19:5–9.

---

12. Paul, *Revelation*, 317.

At the end of chapter 19 there appears to be no one left following the widespread judgment/battle. The answer to the saints' cry in 6:10 is now being fulfilled: "How long O Sovereign Lord, holy and true, until you judge the inhabitants of the earth and avenge our blood?" However, there are two more judgment scenes yet to take place in chapter 20.

SATAN'S JUDGMENT AND THE MILLENNIAL REIGN OF THE SAINTS (CH. 20)

Chapter 20 constitutes a further removal or judgment scene in the form of the judgment of the dragon, Satan (vv. 1–3, 7–10), and the Great White Throne judgment where all things are finally removed (vv. 11–15). In the midst of this is an account of the resurrection and reign of the saints for one thousand years (vv. 4–6). The events recorded in chapter 20 do not necessarily happen chronologically after chapter 19, but are a further series of visions that depict a different perspective on what happens at the coming of Christ at the end of history. The order of events recorded in these chapters refers to the order in which John saw them, not necessarily the order in which they are to occur in time. Furthermore, there is also a literary relationship of chapters 19–20 to chapters 12–13. The dragon and the two beasts introduced in chapters 12–13 are now disposed of in chapters 19–20 in the *reverse order* in which they were introduced. The main theme of chapter 20, then, is the judgment and destruction of the chief antagonist of God and his people: the dragon, Satan.

Satan's judgment takes place in two stages. First, he is locked up in the abyss, the home and prison of demonic, satanic beings (vv. 1–3; see 9:1–2; 11:7). Second, he is let out to be destroyed in a final battle (vv. 7–10). This reflects a common depiction in Jewish and Christian literature

Visions of Judgment and Salvation II (Revelation 17–20)

of how demonic beings will be judged—locked away in a prison of darkness temporarily, to be let out only to go into eternal punishment (1 Enoch 10:4–5, 11–12; 2 Pet 2:4; Jude 6). First, Satan is locked away in the abyss, the home of demonic beings (vv. 1–3). The purpose is so that he is no longer able to deceive the nations, which he has done throughout the book. The period is specified as one thousand years, a number symbolizing completeness and great magnitude. Second, after that time he will be released from the abyss, with the implication that he will be let out to go into final judgment. This act will allow for the next important event: the resurrection and reign of the saints for one thousand years, known as the millennial kingdom (vv. 4–6). There are two main issues in understanding this period of time. What is the significance of the number one thousand, and what is the Millennium's role and function in Revelation? The number one thousand signifies completeness and wholeness, and likely is not to be taken as referring to a literal one-thousand-year period of time. The Millennium has attracted attention in disproportion to the space allotted to it in John's Apocalypse. The church has traditionally interpreted the Millennium in three ways. First, a view that is less common today, known as *Post*millennialism, argues that the Millennium will be a golden age set up on earth through the witnessing of the church and the powerful work of the Holy Spirit. Christ will then return after (hence, *Post-*) that time. A much more common view, known as *A*millennialism, argues that the Millennium symbolizes not a future period of time (hence, *A-*) but the entire church age between the first coming and the second coming of Christ, where Christ and his saints reign from heaven. A third popular view, known as *Pre*millennialism, argues that Christ will return in the future before (hence, *Pre-*) the Millennium to set it up on earth.[13] There is some variety within these positions.

In arriving at an interpretation it is important to pay close attention to how the Millennium functions within the book of Revelation itself. Very little is said in these verses about what actually happens during this time (the saints reign), or even where it takes place (heaven or earth?). Verse 4 also suggests that it is primarily for the martyrs, though the martyrs may represent all the saints, since all God's people presumably participate in the resurrection and all those who overcome in the seven messages in chapters 2–3 will be granted life. The Millennium takes place within the context of Satan's judgment. Satan was described as the accuser of the brother in 12:10. The dragon, Satan, is the one who ruled the world and who put the saints to death. Now in a profound reversal, Satan's activity is curtailed and the saints come to life and they reign, the opposite of the state of affairs under Satan's rule. In other words, now that the guilty party is being judged, those that he wrongly accused and killed are vindicated: They come to life and reign. The meaning of the Millennium is this: the resurrection and vindication of the saints. In the context of Satan's judgment, the saints are not forgotten, especially those who have died for their faithful witness.[14] This vision of the saints' reward provides an interlude in this long series of visions of judgment. The one thousand years is not important for any temporal information it conveys (it probably does not refer to a specific period of time at all), but metaphorically shows the completeness and magnitude of the saints' vindication. The temporal designation "one thousand years" metaphorically contrasts with the much shorter periods of

13. Chung and Mathewson, *Models of Premillennialism*.
14. Fee, *Revelation*, 280–81.

Visions of Judgment and Salvation II (Revelation 17–20)

time that characterize Satan's tyranny and the saints' persecution: three and one-half years, forty-two months, 1260 days. Now the saints reign for a much greater metaphorical period of time. The point of the thousand years is that their vindication will far exceed anything they suffered at the hands of the dragon. The resurrection and vindication of the saints in 20:4–6 will prepare them for life in the new creation of 21:1—22:5.

In another pronouncement of blessing, this event in vv. 4–6 is called the "first resurrection." Those who participate in it will not experience the "second death." But there is no explicit mention of a second resurrection or a first death. Within the context of Revelation, the first death would be physical death that all humanity, including the people of God, will suffer. The second death is identified as the lake of fire, eternal judgment and separation from God, in 20:14. This is the lot of those who have sided with the dragon and whose names do not appear in the book of life. The second resurrection, likely referred to in v. 5 ("the rest of the dead did not come to life until after the thousand years were completed"), then is found in 20:11–15, which is a judgment of unbelievers (those whose names are not in the book of life). So the saints will experience the first death but will not be harmed by the second death, since they will participate in the first resurrection unto eternal life. The followers of the dragon will experience the second resurrection unto judgment and the second death, eternal punishment and separation from God (20:11–15). Following the vindication of the saints, attention turns back to the dragon, who is now let out to go into judgment (vv. 7–10). But on his way there he musters the kings of the earth to participate in another battle. Most likely, this refers to the exact same battle narrated back in 19:11–21, but now from the perspective of the dragon's judgment. The first account of the battle emphasized the destruction of the two beasts from chapter 13. Now for literary effect the author narrates the same battle to emphasize the judgment of the dragon from chapter 12. The same Old Testament text utilized in 19:11–21 also underlies the description of this battle: Ezekiel 38–39. From this text John gets the reference to Gog and Magog (20:8), which symbolize the entire earth and its nations who band together in a final assault against God's people (v. 9). The outcome is the same as in 19:11–20: No fighting takes place as the enemies are simply destroyed in judgment, being consumed by fire. Consequently, the dragon joins the two beasts in the lake of fire, the place of eternal judgment (20:9). The primary antagonists of God and his people in the drama of Revelation have been disposed of to harm the earth and God's people no more.

THE GREAT WHITE THRONE JUDGMENT (20:11–15)

A final "sweeping up" scene records the judgment and removal of all things. The judgment is comprehensive; everything is judged so that nothing remains by the end of chapter 20. This is the second resurrection, and all the dead, both on earth and in the sea, who are not found in the book of life are raised to face judgment before the Great White Throne. This is what was referred to in v. 5, the rest of the dead who come to life after the thousand years. Most likely, this is the (second) resurrection of *unbelievers* to judgment, in the same way that 20:4–6 was the (first) resurrection of *believers* to life in preparation for entering the new creation in chapters 21–22. Moreover, even the present creation is forced to flee in judgment before the presence of the throne. The present earth has been

Visions of Judgment and Salvation II (Revelation 17–20)

the home of the dragon, the beasts, and the kingdom of empires like Rome. So it is also removed in judgment. Everything is now in the lake of fire (v. 15). Chapter 20, then, ends the series of judgment scenes, so that everything that opposes the full realization of God's kingdom is cleared away. All that remains now is the emergence of the new creation in 21:1—22:5.

REFLECTION

1. How might John's visions of the judgment of Babylon-Rome continue to find application beyond the first-century Roman Empire, since the end-time judgment did not occur when first-century Rome fell?

2. What is the focus of John's vision of the Millennium in 20:4–6, given what he says about it and the relatively small space he devotes to us? What does this say about the attention the Millennium has gotten in many groups and churches today?

7

A FINAL VISION OF FUTURE SALVATION: THE NEW CREATION (REVELATION 21-22)

Now that everything that stands as a barrier to the establishment of God's kingdom on earth and his people's enjoyment of it has been removed in a final act of judgment (chs. 19-20), all that remains is the establishment of the new creation and New Jerusalem as the reward for the faithful people of God. The New Jerusalem/bride in chapter 21 stands as the counter-image to the Babylon/prostitute of chapters 17-18. This can be seen by the fact that another angel who had the seven bowl plagues now shows John the New Jerusalem/bride (21:9-10), just as it had shown John the Babylon/prostitute (17:1). If God's people will "come out" of Babylon (18:4), they must have another city they can go to. The new creation in this vision stands as

A Final Vision of Future Salvation

the reward for the seven churches if they will overcome by refusal to compromise with Babylon/Rome and by maintaining their faithful witness (see 2:7, 11, 17, 26–29; 3:5, 12, 21, where features from chapters 20–22 are picked up in the promises to the overcomer). Therefore, the main function of 21:1—22:5 is exhortational, to motivate the churches to refuse to compromise with Rome and remain faithful and obedient so they can enter the New Jerusalem. Revelation 21:1—22:5 is laden with allusions to and echoes from Old Testament prophetic texts.[1] All of God's purposes for his people and for all creation now come to climactic fulfillment in this final vision. While most readings of Revelation throughout church history have privileged the Millennium passage (20:4–6), the density of Old Testament allusions within the textual space of 21:1—22:5 suggests that the consummated new creation should be the focal point of attention. The prophetic anticipations of God restoring his people and dwelling in their midst in a promised Messianic era on earth is now realized in this vision of the consummation of God's redemptive plan for his people and all creation in the new creation of 21:1—22:5.

While Old Testament texts are paramount in importance in this climactic vision, John's vision of the New Jerusalem may also reflect an important Greco-Roman background. That is, the conception of the New Jerusalem in 21:1—22:5 probably also reflects notions of the ideal Greco-Roman city.[2] Features such as aesthetics, symmetry and beauty, a main street running through it, a good water supply, gates for adornment rather than protection,

1. For a comprehensive treatment of the use of the Old Testament in Rev 21:1—22:5 see Mathewson, *New Heaven and a New Earth*.

2. Schüssler Fiorenza, *Revelation: Vision of a Just World*, 113–14; and especially Gilchrest, *Revelation 21-22 in Light of Jewish and Greco-Roman Utopianism*.

and ethnic diversity would have made up typical conceptions of a utopian or ideal Greco-Roman city. These features provide correspondences with the New Jerusalem in 21:1—22:5. By modeling the New Jerusalem on the ideal city and utopian conditions in it, John's point is that the perfect city and society are not fulfilled in the ideal Greco-Roman city, but in the New Jerusalem anticipated in Old Testament prophetic texts and now envisioned in Revelation's final chapters.

PRESENCE AND ABSENCE IN THE NEW CREATION (21:1—22:5)

Following the removal of the first heaven and earth (20:11), John now sees it replaced by a new heaven and earth (21:1, 5) in fulfillment of Isaiah 65:17. The word "new" occurs no less than four times in 21:1–5, emphasizing the qualitative newness of the new order of things. Most likely John envisions the complete renewal and renovation of the old order (21:5), rather than a destruction of it and a totally new creation out of nothing (see Rom 8:20–22).[3] According to Revelation's climactic vision, and consistent with the New Testament insistence on the future resurrection of the saints (see 1 Cor 15; 1 Thess 4:13–18), the final destiny of God's people is a thoroughly physical, earthly existence, albeit transformed and renewed (Rev 21:5). This section of John's vison can be understood through the twin lenses of presence and absence: what will be present in the new creation, and what will be absent.[4]

---

3. Mathewson, *New Heaven and New Earth*, 35–39.

4. Koester also discusses the themes of presence and absence in Rev 21:1—22:5 from a more limited perspective in *Revelation and the End of All Things*, 188–89.

A Final Vision of Future Salvation

Absence in the New Creation

According to 21:1—22:5 there are several things that have no place in the new creation. The first thing that the author says will be absent or "no more" is the sea (21:1c). The sea throughout Revelation often carries negative connotations. The beast comes out of the sea (13:1). The sea is also the home of the dead (20:13). In the ancient world the sea also often carried negative associations. In some Jewish literature the sea was emblematic of chaos and evil (see Ps 74:13–14; Jer 51:36; Nah 1:4; Isa 51:9; Dan 7:2–3; 4 Ezra 6:49–52; 2 Apocalypse of Baruch 29:4; 1 Enoch 60:7–8). Hence, the threatening sea of chaos and evil here is metaphorical for the barrier to the establishment of God's kingdom and the full enjoyment of the new creation by God's people. Moreover, it probably also constitutes part of John's new Exodus motif (see Rev 8–9, 15–16). In the same way that God dried up the Red Sea of evil that threatened and barred Israel's freedom and entrance into the land (see Isa 51:9), so God will once again remove the sea of evil and chaos that bars entrance into the land, the new creation, in Revelation 21:1.[5]

The second thing that will be absent in the new order of things is death, crying, mourning, and pain (21:4). That is because the old order of things, under the dominion of sin, and where the dragon and beasts ruled and brought oppression, suffering, and death to God's people causing pain and tears, has finally been removed.

The third thing that will be absent is anything which or anyone who would bring or do injustice, evil, impurity, and godlessness (21:8, 27) into the new creation. Such things characterized the old order of things. These must all be removed because there is no room for anyone

5. Mathewson, "New Exodus as Background."

or anything that would cause harm, evil, pain, injustice, and destruction of life or bring impurity in God's just and perfect world. This contrasts with the prostitute, Babylon, which was full of abominations (17:5) and which exploited the nations. Their lot is eternal separation from God's presence and life in the new creation in the lake of fire, that is, the second death.

The fourth thing that will be absent from the new creation is a temple (21:22). At the center of the city where John might expect to encounter a temple in his vision, he does not see one. There will be no separate physical temple in the new creation because God and the Lamb now dwell directly with their people. Now that the old creation affected by sin and evil has been removed, which required a temple for God to dwell with his people in the first place, there is no longer a need for it in the new order of things. The goal that the temple symbolized, the unmediated presence of God with his people on earth, has now been fully and perfectly realized with God and the Lamb dwelling directly in the midst of their people in the new creation. The symbol has given way to the reality, so a further physical temple would be redundant. The fifth thing that will be absent in the new creation is the need of the sun and moon (21:23; 22:5). These luminaries which gave light to the old creation are no longer needed since God and the Lamb will be the continuous source of light in the new creation (see below). The presence of the lamp which is the Lamb (21:23) contrasts with Babylon, where the light of the lamp no longer shines (18:23); Babylon dwells in perpetual darkness, the new Jerusalem in perpetual light. The new creation will be so suffused with the glorious light-giving presence of God and the Lamb that that which was needed to give light in the first creation will be unnecessary. This may not necessarily mean that the sun and moon will disappear altogether, but only that they will not be needed, though perhaps still present.[6] As a corollary to the absence of the need of these luminaries, the sixth thing that will be absent in the new creation is night (21:25; 22:5), a motif that John also draws on from prophetic texts (Zech 14:7). The notion of night suggests spiritual darkness, sin, and evil.[7] Darkness could also suggest threat and lack of safety, since this is when a city would be most vulnerable to attack. Because there will be no more darkness, the gates of the city can remain open and the city dwells in perpetual security. The final thing that will be absent in the new creation is a curse (22:3). The absence of the curse may recall the curse on the first creation at the fall (Gen 3:14–17). In addition, the word used here in Revelation 22:3 can also be translated a "ban on destruction," reflecting reliance on Zechariah 14:11. The word referred in the Old Testament to something that was devoted to destruction in warfare. Now, the New Jerusalem never needs to fear destruction by enemies, but dwells in perpetual peace and security.[8]

Presence in the New Creation

Even more important than what will be absent is what will be present in the new order of things. While John may not intentionally be thinking in terms of what is "present" in contrast to what is "absent" in the new creation, it is still helpful to frame the treatment of the main features of the new creation in this way.

---

6. Paul, *Revelation*, 355.
7. Paul, *Revelation*, 356.
8. Mathewson, *New Heaven and New Earth*, 201–3.

The Bride of the Lamb, the New Jerusalem

One of the first things John sees in the new creation is the bride of the Lamb (21:2, 9; Isa 61:10), whose wedding feast was announced back in 19:6–9. Now the wedding between the Lamb and his bride is consummated. The image of a bride contrasts with that of the prostitute in chapters 17–18. The bride imagery suggests purity, faithfulness, and joy. God's intimate relationship with his people is solidified with the establishment of a new covenant (21:3; see Ezek 37:27; Lev 26:27) according to which God will now live with his people. The bride is also identified as the New Jerusalem: John is told by the angel that he is going to be shown the bride of the Lamb (21:9), but then he is shown the New Jerusalem (21:10). The juxtaposition of the bride and the New Jerusalem suggests that it is not so much a reference to a literal city; the New Jerusalem is metaphorical for the people of God themselves. The emphasis is on a people, not a place.[9] The Old Testament anticipates the rebuilding of an end-time Jerusalem (Isa 54, 61, 65), and John now sees the fulfillment of that reality in the consummated people of God themselves. Furthermore, the consummated people of God consist of Old Testament Israel, represented by the twelve gates (21:12–13) as well as the New Testament people of God, the church, founded on the twelve apostles of the Lamb (21:14). In this way, John makes it clear that the people of God are not defined ethnically (Israel), but consist of people from every nation, now belonging to God's people based on their relationship to the Lamb. The measurements of the city are all multiples of twelve, the number of the people of God (twelve tribes of Israel, twelve apostles). There are twelve gates (21:12–13)

---

9. This notion was emphasized by Gundry, "People as Place, Not Place for People."

A Final Vision of Future Salvation

and twelve foundation stones (21:14); the city's length, breadth, and height measure 12,000 cubits; the wall is 144 cubits (12 x 12; high or thick?); the leaves of the tree of life bear twelve kinds of fruit for twelve months (22:2). Again, John's vision is not of a precise architectural blueprint of a literal city, rather it symbolizes the great multitude of the perfected, consummated people of God.

The Presence of God and the Lamb

The most important feature of the end-time new creation is that God and the Lamb are present in the midst of their people (21:11, 23; 22:1, 3). The promise of the new covenant includes God's tabernacle-dwelling directly with his people (21:3). The entire city shines with the glorious presence of God. The precious metal, gold, also suggests a place of divine presence (21:18), and the shape of the city as a cube (21:16) resembles the shape of the Holy of Holies in the Old Testament temple (1 Kgs 6:20), the specific place where God's presence dwelled. John draws extensively on Ezekiel 40–48 in 21:1—22:5, but whereas Ezekiel sees and measures a temple, John sees and measures the entire city-people. The entire New Jerusalem is a temple where God's presence resides.[10] The fact that God's presence suffuses the entire city explains the absence of the temple (21:21). The physical temple symbolized the presence of God with his people. Now the symbol has given way to the reality,[11] the unmediated presence of God is with his people, rendering a separate structure no longer necessary (see above). The life-giving presence of God and the Lamb, represented as

---

10. Therefore, Rev 21:1—22:5 is the culmination of the process of "building" the temple of God begun in Eph 2:20-22; 1 Pet 2:5.

11. Schüssler Fiorenza, *Revelation: Vision of a Just World*, 112.

glorious light (see below), permeates the entire city, and all have immediate access to it. This feature is the focal point of life in the new creation: "God with us."

The Throne of God and the Lamb

The presence of God and the Lamb is also indicated by the presence of the throne at the center of the new creation (22:1, 3). The throne which was in heaven in chapters 4–5 now comes down to earth. God's will and kingdom which were realized in heaven have now finally been realized on a renewed earth (see Matt 6:9–10). The throne, primarily a political symbol, is a symbol of God's and the Lamb's kingship and sovereignty over all things. As such, it functions as a counterclaim to Imperial Roman rule. At the center of the new creation stands the just reign and rule of God. This contrasts with the abuse of power by Babylon's reign and rule which stood at the center of the first creation (18:7). By contrast, God's power and rule issue in life, healing, and justice in the renewed world. Furthermore, God's people will also share in his rule in the new creation (22:5).

Precious stones

John describes the makeup of the New Jerusalem as consisting of a variety of precious stones. Overall, the impression this gives is of the incomparable beauty, splendor, preciousness, and purity of the city. The precious stones are part of the attire of the adorned bride/New Jerusalem (21:2; see Isa 54:11–12) and they contrast with their gaudy display on the prostitute/Babylon (17:4). In addition to the adornment of the bride, the presence of precious stones also indicates that the city reflects God's glory, since one of the jewels in particular—jasper in 21:11, 18—is found in

A Final Vision of Future Salvation

the throne room scene in 4:3, signifying God's glory and presence throughout the city. The gates are made of pearl (21:21) and the entire city and its street are made of gold that is transparent like glass (21:18, 21). The New Jerusalem is a place that shines with the beauty and splendor of God's glory. The twelve precious stones, which make up the twelve foundations (21:14, 19–20) also represent the stones on the breastplate of the high priest (Exod 28:17–20). The entire city is a temple, and its people are priests who reflect God's presence. The impression the reader gets is that the entire city shimmers with the beauty and glorious light of God's and the Lamb's presence. It may also suggest that the wealth that was ostentatiously displayed and exploited by Babylon has been redeemed in the New Jerusalem, and all have access to it (not just the wealthy elite).

The Kings and Nations

Perhaps one of the most surprising features present in the new creation is the kings of the earth and nations. They enter the city and bring their glory into it (21:24, 26). The leaves on the tree of life in 22:2 are explicitly said to be for the healing of the nations (see below). In the previous chapters of Revelation the kings and the nations have generally been portrayed in a negative light, as hostile to the people of God and deceived by and in league with the dragon, Satan, and the two beasts (11:9–10; 13:7; 17:1, 15; 19:15; 20:8). In chapters 19–20 the kings and nations have been completely destroyed in judgment (19:17–21; 20:7–10), leaving the reader to ponder their presence in the New Jerusalem.[12] The presence of the nations and kings in the New Jerusalem following their description as

12. Mathewson, "The Destiny of the Nations."

in alliance with the beasts and their total destruction in judgment is likely highly rhetorical. First, it emphasizes the complete transfer of the kingdom of Satan and of this world to God and the Lamb in order to emphasize the complete and universal authority of God and the Lamb. This world, including the nations, are no longer subservient to Babylon and to the beast, but to God and the Lamb; hence, the presence of the nations in the new creation. Second, the tension shows the options open to the nations, either salvation or judgment. Third, the tension also emphasizes the complete judgment of God, and the complete salvation. John's intention is not to show quantitatively how many from the nations will receive judgment or salvation. Fourth, John alludes to Old Testament prophetic texts which expect an end-time conversion of the nations (Isa 2:2–4; 60). Consistent with this, John's picture of eschatological salvation includes the nations and kings of the earth as God's kingdom now comes to earth. The nations, which offered their glory and allegiance to the beast, now give glory to God (11:13; 14:7; 15:4).[13]

Light

The obvious corollary to the absence of darkness in the new creation is the presence of light (21:11, 23, 24; 22:5). We have already noted that the New Jerusalem is so suffused with the radiant presence of God that the luminaries in this creation are no longer needed with no more nighttime (21:23; 22:5). The new creation will be characterized by unending light. Light is a metaphor for God's presence. It also suggests the salvation that God provides. Once more, the picture created is of the new creation and New

13. Bauckham, *Climax of Prophecy*, 315.

A Final Vision of Future Salvation

Jerusalem completely suffused with the life-giving, illuminating, and saving presence of God that all in the new creation now have direct access to.

The Garden-Paradise

The establishment of a new creation will also mean a return of paradise conditions (22:1-2) from Genesis 1-2. The end will be as the beginning. The precious stones and gold in the New Jerusalem may evoke the motif of paradise, since gold, jewels, and precious metals featured in the first paradise (Gen 2:11-12), and in Ezekiel 28:13 the precious stones on the breastplate are worn by Adam in the garden. The two most explicit paradise motifs are the river of life (22:1) and the tree of life (22:2). The river of life in v. 1 draws from Ezekiel 47:1, which also reflects the river that flowed from the garden of Eden in Genesis 2:10. That is, the new city is the source of unending life for the people of God, who spiritually drink from the living water (21:6). Most likely, the water of life is a metaphor for the Holy Spirit, who gives life to the people of God; the association of water and the Holy Spirit is made elsewhere in Johannine literature (John 7:37-39).[14] The fact that the water of life is available "without cost" (21:6) contrasts with the exploitative and unbalanced economy of the Roman Empire. The tree of life is also present at the center of the New Jerusalem (22:2; see Ezek 47:12; Gen 2:9). It too gives unending life (it produces fruit every month) to the people of God in the new creation. The tree of life in v. 2 is also said to have leaves that provide healing for the nations. The nations that were seduced by the prostitute, Babylon and

---

14. See the commentaries by Swete, Wilcock, Mangina, Williamson, Paul.

deceived by the dragon, and even hostile to God's people, now find healing in the New Jerusalem.

In a climactic vision full of rich symbols and images, the new creation in Revelation 21:1—22:5, is the final goal of the long process of redemptive history, anticipated in the Old Testament prophetic texts, fulfilled in Jesus and his people, and now reaching its climax in God and the Lamb dwelling with their people in a new creation. The new creation will be the establishment of God's perfect and just world, characterized by unending light and life. God's people will function as kings and priests (22:4-5), fulfilling the role that Adam and Eve were to fulfill in the first creation (Gen 1:26-28) but failed to do because of disobedience. Now as priests God's people are in his presence and see his face (22:4) and they rule over the new creation forever (22:5).

CONCLUDING WORDS (22:6-21)

Revelation now moves from vision to concluding epistolary reflections on what John has seen, with final instructions for reading and obeying the book. The very last verse (22:21) encases the entire work within an epistolary framework (with 1:4-6). John's visionary world of fantastic images and metaphors now gives way to a return to the world of ordinary life, but a world now perceived through the lenses of what John has just seen in 4:1—22:5.[15] This section concludes the entire vision by emphasizing a number of themes that have been important in the previous chapters.

---

15. Koester, *Revelation and the End of All Things*, 197.

A Final Vision of Future Salvation

Jesus' Soon Return

These closing verses of Revelation remind the reader of the nearness of Christ's return to consummate God's redemptive purposes. Three times in this section a voice in the first person promises, "I am coming soon" (vv. 7, 12, 20). The speaker is Christ in all three instances, and here he claims to be coming back soon to bring to consummation the vision that John was just shown in the previous chapters. Once John is told that the "time is near" (v. 10). This is the reason that, in contrast to Daniel 12:4, John is told not to seal up the book of Revelation (22:10). It is a message for his contemporary readers, not for some distant and future generation. By claiming to come soon, Jesus emphasizes the temporal and spatial nearness of his return for his people. John is not predicting that Jesus will come in his lifetime (and then was mistaken). Rather, John writes from the perspective that Christ's first coming and his death and resurrection have already inaugurated the end, so that Christ could return at any time to consummate God's purposes for his creation. John's concern is the certainty that Jesus *will* return, not *when* he will return. The emphasis on Christ's soon return in vv. 6–21 has a hortatory purpose (v. 7), to instill vigilance and holy living in God's people in view of the soon return of the one who will bring the salvation and judgment depicted in the rest of the book.[16] Therefore, the church (and John) responds by praying for the return of Christ to consummate God's purposes (vv. 17, 20).

---

16. Mathewson, *Where is the Promise of His Coming?*

The Words of Jesus

The book begins and closes with reminders that what John has written in his book is the very words of Jesus; they are not John's own, and therefore must be taken with the utmost seriousness. The words John writes are "trustworthy and true" because the Lord himself is the one who inspires the prophets (v. 6). In v. 16 Jesus is the one who testifies to what is written in the book of Revelation. And again, the section ends with Jesus testifying to everything seen and written in the book (v. 20). This is meant to authenticate the prophetic words of John and give them authority, so that the readers will be encouraged to obey them.

The True Object of Worship

The closing verses remind the reader of the only appropriate response to what John has seen and what the readers have read in the preceding vision. Verses 6–9 end the vision of the New Jerusalem in the same way that the vision of the prostitute/Babylon ended (19:9–10): John falls down to worship the angel who has showed him this vision, but is told to worship only God. This is a major theme of the book: Who is worthy of worship? Who is seated on the throne and in control of all things? The only true object of worship is God (and the Lamb) seated on the throne at the center of all reality (see chs. 4–5). To give such allegiance to anyone or anything else is idolatry, even to exalted angelic beings.

Who Jesus Is

There is a renewed affirmation in this final section of who Jesus is, the one who has been the main character

A Final Vision of Future Salvation

of the book (see ch. 5), who authenticates these words of prophecy, and who will return soon to bring to completion God's redemptive purposes. Revelation ends with a reassertion that Christ is the "Alpha and Omega, the First and the Last, the Beginning and the End" (v. 12b). Jesus is the one who stands at the beginning and end of this book (see 1:17) and at the beginning and end of history. Therefore, he will bring history to its goal in his soon return (v. 12a). The one who shares in God's eternal being and identity is the one who can bring God's purposes to their final fulfillment. Jesus is also the "root and offspring of David" (v. 16), identifying him as the one who brings to fulfillment all of the Old Testament promises of a coming Davidic ruler who will rule the nations and bring salvation and God's kingdom to earth. He is also the "bright and morning star" (v. 16; see 2:28), for in Jesus the new age of salvation is dawning for his people. God's people therefore have every reason to follow Christ in obedience and confidence that he will bring God's redemptive purposes for all creation to their intended goal.

Prophetic Warning and Encouragement

All of the above themes function to offer prophetic warning and encouragement for the people of God. This is the primary function of the prophetic genre (see ch. 1, "Reading the Book of Revelation"). The entire book of Revelation is framed with a call to "keep" (obey) the words of John's prophecy (1:3; 22:7). The promise that Jesus is coming soon is to motivate the readers to keep the words of the prophecy (v. 7) because at that time Jesus will reward those who have been faithful (v. 12). Verse 14 pronounces another blessing (see v. 7) on the one who remains faithful and holy, for they will participate in the new creation of

21:1—22:5. But those who live ungodly lives and practice the vices of v. 15 will find themselves excluded from the new creation. Yet the invitation remains open for all to drink from the water of life (v. 17). The eschatological life of the new creation (22:2) is already available to anyone who will accept it. The warning not to add to and subtract from the book of Revelation in vv. 18–19 is probably also to be understood as a call to obedience. The language of "adding" and "subtracting" comes from Deuteronomy 4:2; 12:32, which warned God's people to be careful to keep everything in the Mosaic Law under the old covenant. Now under the new covenant, John uses this language of adding to and subtracting from metaphorically to refer to failing to obey Revelation's prophetic words. The readers add to and subtract from Revelation by refusing to maintain their faithful witness and by compromising with the pagan empire.[17] Those that disobey will find themselves the object of God's plague-judgments throughout the book and will find themselves excluded from the promised new creation. Therefore, the entire book of Revelation is bookended with both blessing for "hearing and keeping" the words of Revelation (21:3; see also 22:7) and cursing for "hearing and failing to keep" the words of Revelation (22:18–19). The divine authentication of John's prophetic words as the words of Jesus (vv. 6, 16) adds force to John's call for obedience. As God's people await the soon return of Christ to bring history to its goal and God's promises to their culmination, in a final epistolary benediction John prays that God's grace will sustain them as they wait for the imminent return of Christ (v. 21): "The grace of the Lord Jesus Christ be with God's people. Amen."

---

17. See especially Beale, *Book of Revelation*, 1150–54; Trafton, *Reading Revelation*, 217.

A Final Vision of Future Salvation

REFLECTION

1. How does the physical nature of the new creation challenge common conceptions of the future hope often held by Christians ("Are you going to heaven?")?

2. Given the transcultural nature of the consummated people of God, what role do you think ethnic distinctions will play in the new creation?

3. Though Revelation 21:1—22:5 does not address all the questions we have about our future hope, how would you summarize what it does say about life in the new creation?

8

THE RELEVANCE OF REVELATION FOR THE CHURCH TODAY

REVELATION HAS EVOKED A variety of responses from its readers throughout church history. For many Christians today, Revelation is still a sealed book, even though John was told not to seal up his book (22:10). Revelation is therefore a book to be avoided, with all its strange images and bizarre content; it is too difficult to understand and should be left to the specialist to decipher. Christians then often retreat to the safer ground of the Gospels or Paul's letters. But Revelation promises a blessing to the one who hears and keeps (obeys) it (1:3). That is, Revelation has a message that is to be obeyed, and in obeying it there is blessing: the promises of eschatological salvation found throughout the book. If Revelation is the word of God that is to be obeyed, God's people can hardly afford to ignore it any more than they can any other biblical book.

The Relevance of Revelation for the Church Today

On the other end of the spectrum, Revelation is often read out of fascination for what it says about the future, sometimes even to the point of obsession, and sometimes with drastic consequences. For such readers Revelation primarily is a source for eschatological speculation and understanding how God is going to bring history to its close. In addition, based on perceived correspondences between what is going on in our modern word—politically, technologically, religiously—and the visions of Revelation, some attempt to plot our existence in relationship to the end, given how Revelation's images are presumably being fulfilled in our own day. The book of Revelation becomes a code to be cracked in light of what is going on in our modern-day world, with the corresponding conclusion that we must be living at the very brink of the end, and Christ's return will happen at any moment, perhaps in our lifetime. However, in the very first chapter of this companion volume we saw that Revelation if anything else must have been comprehensible to its first-century audience, not a message hidden until a later (e.g., twenty-first-century) generation finally discovers its true meaning. Instead, John's book was trying to help specific churches living in the first-century Roman Empire (chs. 2–3) make sense of their world. John wrote to challenge the churches to maintain their faithful witness in a hostile environment, no matter what the consequences it might bring (persecution, or even martyrdom). So if the book of Revelation was primarily a message for first-century readers living in the shadow of the Roman Empire, and not a code that we can now finally unlock in the twenty-first century, what is the ongoing relevance of the book of Revelation for the people of God today?

A CONTRIBUTION TO EVERY MAJOR AREA OF CHRISTIAN DOCTRINE

With an obsession with the eschatology in Revelation, most Christian readers of Revelation miss the important fact that Revelation makes an important, and even sometimes unique, contribution to virtually every major area of Christian doctrine; eschatology is probably not the most important doctrine in Revelation. Without Revelation our theology would be somewhat impoverished. Therefore, Revelation should play a role in the confession of the church. The following touches on only some of the more important theological themes that receive extensive development in John's Apocalypse.[1]

God. Revelation is a highly theocentric book.[2] At its center stands a vision of God who is the just, holy, and sovereign creator of all things (ch. 4). God and his throne are at the center of reality, and all things are oriented to God in worship. All human authority is displaced. As the alpha and omega, God stands at the beginning and end of all things as the eternal one. He is the originator of creation and its goal. The image of the One seated on the throne emphasizes God's sovereignty and his intention to set up his sovereignty and rule over all that oppose it. His sovereignty perfectly realized in heaven must become a reality on earth. God will return to judge the entire created world in truth and justice. God is transcendent and stands above his creation, yet he is imminently present in it in the form of the Lamb to bring redemption to his people, and will reside with his people in the new creation.

---

1. For a full treatment of Revelation's theology, see Bauckham, *Theology of Revelation*.
2. Bauckham, *Theology of Revelation*, 23.

Christ. God's redemptive purposes for humanity and all of history are accomplished through Jesus Christ. Christ's role is to bring about the establishment of God's kingdom on earth. The most characteristic image used to describe Jesus is the slaughtered Lamb. Christ is the one that through his death purchases people for God. His death is also a model for his followers—they overcome in the same way he did, through suffering even to the point of death. Revelation assumes Jesus' humanity; he is the child born to the woman; he is of the tribe of Judah and the root of Jesse, the Christ, and hence the fulfillment of Israel's coming messianic ruler; and he died as the sacrificial Lamb. Yet Revelation also has a "high" Christology, emphasizing the deity of Christ perhaps more than any other New Testament book. Jesus shares in the identity and eternal being of God. He sits on the same throne as God and is worthy of the same worship, and he shares the title that indicates eternity: "First and Last, Alpha and Omega, Beginning and End." The work of Christ also gets attention in the book. His sacrificial death on the cross as a slain Lamb is the price for providing redemption for his people. His resurrection defeats evil and death, and it guarantees the resurrection of his followers. Jesus is God's agent of judgment, and will one day return to judge the entire world. He is already present with his churches, but will be physically present with his people in the new creation.

People of God/Church. The people of God in Revelation take the form of seven historical churches in ancient Asia Minor. The church is encouraged to maintain its faithful witness and resist the temptation to compromise with the pagan world. A variegated imagery characterizes the church in John's Apocalypse. The church is a multicultural people that have been redeemed from every tribe, language, people, and nation. They are a kingdom and God's priests in this world, representing God's presence and rule. They are a mighty army that goes out to do battle through their faithful and suffering witness. They overcome the world by their faithful witness to the truth in the face of suffering and death. They are the true temple of God, protected by God even though subject to physical harm at the hands of the dragon and beast. But God's people will enter the new creation and constitute a temple-city where God dwells directly in their midst. They are two witnesses who witness to the reality of God's purposes in the world and the truth of the Gospel, again in the face of opposition and suffering. They are the bride of the Lamb, the consummated people of God. Overall, the church in Revelation is called to maintain a faithful witness in a hostile world, and they do so in the face of suffering, even to the point of death.

Salvation. Christ's death on the cross is the price that redeems people from sin, death, and from the reign of the powers of evil. God's people are redeemed to be a kingdom of priests for God. Yet salvation in Revelation has a clear eschatological dimension. God's people will participate in the end-time resurrection to life (already anticipated with Christ's own resurrection) and they will inherit the new creation. Hence, salvation in Revelation has a clear physical dimension. One of the ways salvation is conceived of in Revelation is through the lens of the Exodus. In the same way he did in the days of the Exodus, God has liberated his people through the sacrifice of a Passover Lamb, Jesus Christ. He liberates his people from sin and from the hostile powers of evil in order to lead them into their promised inheritance, the new creation.

Eschatology. Though eschatology is not the overarching concern of Revelation's visions, Revelation does have more to say than any other book about the ultimate fulfillment of God's purposes for history and his people. Revelation is clear that history is moving towards a goal—the second coming of Christ to bring God's redemptive purposes to their consummation. The following is a description of the main contours of Revelation's eschatology. Jesus Christ's death and resurrection have inaugurated the end-time promises of God's kingdom and new creation. Yet, God's people still await the ultimate consummation (chs. 19–22). The present age spanning the period of the church's existence between the first and second coming of Christ is a time of tribulation, where the dragon and the beasts wage war on the people of God, those redeemed by the sacrificial death of the Lamb. God's people are called to persevere and maintain their faithful witness, even if it means suffering and death. During this time, God and the Lamb will also pour out their preliminary judgments (seals, trumpets) on the earth, in anticipation of the final judgment yet to come (bowls, Babylon, final battle). Christ will bring this period of tribulation (symbolized by three and one-half years, forty-two months, and 1260 days) to an end with his second coming. At his second coming Christ will judge and remove everything that opposes the establishment of his just and perfect rule in a new creation and his people's enjoyment of it. In the midst of this he will resurrect, vindicate, and reward his people (20:4–6) for their suffering and faithful witness. Once everything has been removed in judgment, God will renew the present creation where he will dwell directly with his people in a new covenant relationship in a new creation (ch. 21). The saints will rule over the new creation with God and the Lamb forever (22:1–5). Beyond this broad structure, the church has tolerated a diversity of approaches to many details that surround this basic outline. Revelation is not interested in providing the kind of details that would permit us to construct any kind of a detailed end-time outline of events.

A CALL TO WORSHIP

When the reader focuses solely on eschatology, there is a danger of missing the fact that Revelation is mainly a book about worship. Revelation answers the question, Who is really in control? Who is deserving of worship and allegiance? God's people primarily relate to God through their worship. The significance of the theme of worship can be seen by the hymnic material scattered throughout the book, where various persons and groups sing hymns of praise. But at the center of the theme of worship is the throne-room scene in ch. 4. Heaven is a place where God's sovereignty is perfectly acknowledged, and all heaven worships God who is seated on the throne. However, Revelation includes another object of worship in ch. 5—the Lamb. Both God and the Lamb receive the worship of heaven equally, without violating Jewish monotheism. The hymns make clear why they are worshiped. In ch. 4 God is worshiped because he is the sovereign creator of all that exists. In ch. 5, God and the Lamb are both worshiped because they have acted to redeem that creation. And one day the entire creation will be a place full of God's and the Lamb's glory where God and the Lamb are worshiped (21:1—22:5). In Revelation, God and Christ are worshiped, not because they need it, but simply because they are worthy, since God is the creator of all and, through the Lamb, the redeemer of all. To give anyone or anything else the worship that only God and the Lamb deserve is idolatry. Revelation should continue to inspire the church's worship today for the same reason: God is the sovereign creator and, through the Lamb, the redeemer. Thus, it places at the center of the vision of God's people the appropriate object and reason for worship. When the church worships, its joins with heaven in acknowledging God's sovereignty as creator and redeemer; the heavenly scene in chapters 4–5 becomes a reality on earth in the church's worship and anticipates the day when all creation will worship God and the Lamb (chs. 21–22). Given its emphasis on worship, it is no wonder that Revelation has inspired the lyrics of a number of the church's worship songs, both old and new.[3] It should continue to inspire the church's worship.

A CALL TO MISSION

As seen above, the church is called to maintain its faithful witness in the world. The dual images of the church as faithful witness and the situation of the nations under the sway of the beast together suggest the importance of mission in Revelation. It is through the faithful witness of the church that the nations are drawn to the truth of the gospel and become the people of God. The vision of the new creation is a vision of a universal people, with the nations coming to the New Jerusalem. This vision should inspire and be reflected in the church's mission to win the nations, those from every tribe, language, and people, through their faithful witness to the truth of God's word and the reality of God's presence. The church is to be a kingdom of priests, who mediate God's presence in the world and are an "outpost" of God's rule and kingdom here on earth.

3. Examples of this include "Holy, Holy, Holy"; Handel's *Messiah*; "Revelation Song"; "Your Great Name"; "Is He Worthy?", to name just a few.

Thus, Revelation is a call to the church to fulfill the universal mission of God to bring salvation to all the nations. As Revelation makes clear, the church carries out its mission in the face of opposition and suffering.

A CALL TO FAITHFUL OBEDIENCE AND DISCIPLESHIP

The primary function of Revelation is hortatory, not to satisfy end-time curiosity. That is, Revelation is a call to faithful obedience, no matter what the consequences. As a prophecy, the book of Revelation functions to give prophetic warning and encouragement. The book is framed with blessing for those who hear and keep (obey) the book of Revelation. In the messages to the seven churches the church is called to repent from compromise and to overcome. God's people are those who keep the commandments of Jesus. Revelation summarizes what it means to be a disciple or follower of Jesus Christ in 14:4: The people of God follow the Lamb wherever he goes. Revelation makes it clear that to follow the Lamb means to obey, but also to go the path of sacrifice and suffering, just as Jesus did. Scattered throughout the book are calls to perseverance and steadfastness. God's people persevere in obedience to Jesus Christ, no matter what the consequences they might face. They refuse to compromise, no matter how enticing the alternative the world offers them. Even the visions of end-time judgment and salvation are meant to inspire perseverance in obedience. Eschatology serves sanctification in Revelation.

The Relevance of Revelation for the Church Today

A CRITIQUE OF GODLESS AND UNJUST EMPIRES

Revelation functions as a prophetic critique of all that was wrong with the first-century Roman Empire in order to warn Christians against compromising with it. Revelation provides a sustained ideological critique of Rome: Rome was guilty of being godless, unjust, violent, and idolatrous, and it usurped divine authority, claiming allegiance and worship that belonged only to God. It had an insatiable desire for power and prosperity. For these reasons Rome would be judged, and all those complicit in its sins. Revelation continues to serve as a critique of any nation, empire, or government that would choose to fall in step with Babylon and reflect its values. As an Apocalypse, the book of Revelation functions to unveil the true nature of reality and what lies behind the godless, evil world system. It exposes the pretensions of any modern-day empire or nation that would play the role of the prostitute-Babylon. It calls on God's people to resist those who perpetrate such evil and injustice through their faithful witness to the truth. Revelation has a concern for social justice, not so much by calling God's people to care for the poor and disenfranchised, but by exposing the ideology behind injustice in our world: violence, arrogance, idolatry, and godlessness. For many readers, it will hit uncomfortably close to home, lest we miss the fact that our own nation or people may reflect the values of Babylon. Revelation, then, serves as a warning not to compromise with such a system, since it will eventually be judged for the same reason Rome-Babylon was. Revelation offers a counter vision to Babylon of a just, perfect world in the vision of the future New Jerusalem. This vision should already be reflected in the life of God's people in the present.

AN INSPIRATION FOR HOPE IN THE PEOPLE OF GOD

The visions of future judgment and salvation, especially of a new creation, should inspire hope in the people of God. History is moving towards a goal—the fulfillment of God's redemptive purposes. One day God will fix all that is wrong with this present world full of evil, injustice, pain, and death. This should inspire hope in God's people, but should also inspire God's people to live out the values of God's kingdom in the present world of injustice, violence, and evil.

REFLECTION

1. What other theological themes do you find in Revelation that you might add to the list above? What does Revelation contribute to our understanding of those themes?

2. Which of the above areas of relevance do you think is most pertinent to the church today?

BIBLIOGRAPHY

Allan, Garrick V., et al., eds. *The Book of Revelation*. Wissenschaftliche Untersuchungen zum Neuen Testament 2. Reihe 411. Tübingen: Mohr Siebeck, 2015.

Aune, David E. "The Form and Function of the Proclamations to the Seven Churches (Revelation 2–3)." *New Testament Studies* 36 (1990) 182–204.

———. *Revelation 1–5*. Word Biblical Commentary 52a. Dallas: Word, 1997.

———. *Revelation 6–16*. Word Biblical Commentary 52b. Nashville: Thomas Nelson, 1998.

———. *Revelation 17–22*. Word Biblical Commentary 52c. Nashville: Thomas Nelson, 1998.

Barr, David L. *Tales of the End: A Narrative Commentary on the Book of Revelation*. Santa Rosa: Polebridge, 1998.

Bauckham, Richard. *The Climax of Prophecy: Studies on the Book of Revelation*. Edinburgh: T&T Clark, 1993.

———. *The Theology of the Book of Revelation*. New Testament Theology. Cambridge: Cambridge University Press, 1993.

Beale, Gregory K. *The Book of Revelation*. New International Greek Testament Commentary. Grand Rapids: Eerdmans, 1999.

———. *John's Use of the Old Testament in Revelation*. JSNT Supplements 166. Sheffield: Sheffield Academic, 1998.

Bibliography

Blount, Brian K. *Revelation: A Commentary*. The New Testament Library. Louisville: Westminster John Knox, 2009.

Boxall, Ian. *The Revelation of Saint John*. Black's New Testament Commentaries. Peabody, MA: Hendrickson, 2006.

Charlesworth, James H., ed. *The Old Testament Pseudepigrapha: Volume 1*. Apocalyptic Literature and Testaments. Garden City, NY: Doubleday, 1983.

Chung, Sung Wook, and David L. Mathewson. *Models of Premillennialism*. Eugene, OR: Cascade, 2018.

Culy, Martin M. *The Book of Revelation: The Rest of the Story*. Eugene, OR: Pickwick, 2017.

deSilva, David A. *Seeing Things John's Way: The Rhetoric of the Book of Revelation*. Louisville: Westminster John Knox, 2009.

———. *Unholy Allegiances: Heeding Revelation's Warning*. Peabody, MA: Hendrickson, 2013.

Fee, Gordon D. *Revelation*. New Covenant Commentary Series 18. Eugene, OR: Cascade, 2011.

Fee, Gordon D., and Douglas Stuart. *How to Read the Bible for All Its Worth*. 3rd ed. Grand Rapids: Zondervan, 2003.

Fekkes, Jan. *Isaiah and Prophetic Traditions in the Book of Revelation: Visionary Antecedents and Their Development*. JSNT Supplements 93. Sheffield: Sheffield Academic, 1994.

Friesen, Steven J. *Imperial Cults and the Apocalypse of John: Reading Revelation in the Ruins*. Oxford: Oxford University Press, 2001.

Gilchrest, Eric J. *Revelation 21–22 in Light of Jewish and Greco-Roman Utopianism*. Biblical Interpretation Series 118. Leiden: Brill, 2013.

Gorman, Michael. *Reading Revelation Responsibly: Uncivil Worship and Witness: Following the Lamb into the New Creation*. Eugene, OR: Cascade, 2011.

Grabiner, Steven. *Revelation's Hymns: Commentary on the Cosmic Conflict*. Library of New Testament Studies 511. London: T&T Clark, 2015.

Gundry, Robert H. "The New Jerusalem: People as Place, Not Place for People." *Novum Testamentum* 29 (1987) 254–62.

Hemer, Colin. *The Letters to the Seven Churches of Asia in Their Local Setting*. JSNT Supplements 11. Sheffield: Sheffield Academic, 1989.

Howard-Brook, Wes, and Anthony Gwyther. *Unveiling Empire: Reading Revelation Then and Now*. Maryknoll, NY: Orbis, 2000.

Klein, William W., et al. *Introduction to Biblical Interpretation*. 3rd ed. Grand Rapids: Zondervan, 2017.

Bibliography

Koester, Craig R. *Revelation and the End of All Things*. 2nd ed. Grand Rapids: Eerdmans, 2001.

———. *Revelation: A New Translation with Introduction and Commentary*. The Anchor Yale Bible 38a. New Haven: Yale University Press, 2014.

Kovacs, Judith, and Christopher Rowland. *Revelation*. Blackwell Bible Commentaries. Oxford: Blackwell, 2004.

Leithart, Peter. *Revelation 1–11*. International Theological Commentary. London: T&T Clark, 2018.

———. *Revelation 12–22*. International Theological Commentary. London: T&T Clark, 2018.

Mangina, Joseph L. *Revelation*. Brazos Theological Commentary on the Bible. Grand Rapids: Brazos, 2010.

Mathewson, David L. "The Destiny of the Nations in Revelation 21:1–22:5: A Reconsideration." *Tyndale Bulletin* 53.1 (2002) 121–42.

———. "New Exodus as a Background for 'The Sea Was No More' in Revelation 21:1c." *Trinity Journal* 24 (2003) 243–58.

———. *A New Heaven and a New Earth: The Meaning and Function of the Old Testament in Revelation 21:1–22:5*. JSNT Supplements 238. London: Sheffield Academic, 2003.

———. "Revelation in Recent Genre Criticism: Some Implications for Interpretation." *Trinity Journal* 13 (1992) 193–213.

———. "Social Justice in the Book of Revelation: Reading Revelation from Above." In *The Bible and Social Justice: Old Testament and New Testament Foundations for the Church's Urgent Call*, 176–97. McMaster New Testament Studies. Eugene, OR: Pickwick, 2015.

———. *Where is the Promise of His Coming? The Delay of the Parousia in the New Testament*. Eugene, OR: Cascade, 2018.

McNicol, Allan J. *The Conversion of the Nations in Revelation*. Library of New Testament Studies 438. London: T&T Clark, 2011.

Morales, Jon. *Christ, Shepherd of the Nations: The Nations as Narrative Character and Audience in John's Apocalypse*. Library of New Testament Studies 577. London: T&T Clark, 2018.

Mounce, Robert H. *The Book of Revelation*. New International Commentary on the New Testament. Grand Rapids: Eerdmans, 1977.

Moyise, Steven. *The Old Testament in the Book of Revelation*. JSNT Supplements 115. Sheffield: Sheffield Academic, 1995.

———, ed. *Studies in the Book of Revelation*. Edinburgh: T&T Clark, 2002.

Bibliography

Ngundu, Onesimus. "Revelation." In *Africa Bible Commentary*, edited by Tokunboh Adeyemo, 1569–605. Grand Rapids: Zondervan, 2006.

Osborne, Grant R. *Revelation*. Baker Exegetical Commentary on the New Testament. Grand Rapids: Baker Academic, 2002.

Paul, Ian. *Revelation*. Tyndale New Testament Commentaries. Downers Grove: IVP Academic, 2018.

Resseguie, James L. *The Revelation of John: A Narrative Commentary*. Grand Rapids: Baker Academic, 2009.

Schüssler Fiorenza, Elisabeth. *Revelation: Vision of a Just World*. Proclamation Commentaries. Minneapolis: Fortress, 1991.

Smalley, Stephen S. *The Revelation to John: A Commentary on the Greek Text of the Apocalypse*. Downers Grove: IVP, 2005.

Swete, Henry B. *The Apocalypse of St. John*. London: Macmillan, 1906.

Thompson, Leonard L. *The Book of Revelation: Apocalypse and Empire*. Oxford: Oxford University Press, 1990.

Trafton, Joseph L. *Reading Revelation: A Literary and Theological Commentary*. Macon, GA: Smyth & Helwys, 2005.

Vanni, Ugo. "Liturgical Dialogue as a Literary Form in the Book of Revelation." *New Testament Studies* 37 (1991) 348–72.

Wilcock, Michael. *The Message of Revelation: I Saw Heaven Opened*. The Bible Speaks Today. Downers Grove: InterVarsity, 1975.

Williamson, Peter S. *Revelation*. Catholic Commentary on Sacred Scripture. Grand Rapids: Baker Academic, 2015.

Wilson, Mark. *Victory through the Lamb*. Wooster, OH: Weaver, 2014.

Witherington, Ben, III. *Revelation*. Cambridge: Cambridge University Press, 2003.

Yarbro Collins, Adela. *The Combat Myth in the Book of Revelation*. Harvard Dissertation Series 9. Missoula: Scholars, 1976.

———. *Crisis and Catharsis: The Power of the Apocalypse*. Philadelphia: Westminster, 1984.

SCRIPTURE INDEX

OLD TESTAMENT/ HEBREW BIBLE

Genesis

1–2	19, 127
1:26–28	128
2:9	127
2:10	127
2:11–12	127
3:14–17	121
3:15	89
15:5	77
22:17–18	77
49:9–10	65

Exodus

6–11	33
7–12	79
7–11	95
10:1–20	80
15	95
28:17–20	125

Leviticus

26:27	122

Numbers

2	76
3:3	34
22–24	50

Deuteronomy

4:2	132
8:2	34
12:32	132
20	93
23:9–10	93

1 Samuel

21:5	93

SCRIPTURE INDEX

2 Samuel

11:11	93

1 Kings

6:20	123
18–19	51

Psalms

2:9	51, 87, 109
74:13–14	119

Isaiah

2:2–4	126
2:10	75
2:19	75
2:21	75
6	44, 58
6:3	62
11:1	65
13:10	75
21:9	103
22	53
23:14–18	98
25:6–8	107
25:8	78
34:4	75
41:10	78
44:6	33
44:9–20	33
47:7–8	102
49:10	78
51:9	119
54	122
54:1–8	107
54:11–12	33, 124
60–62	107
60	126
61	122
61:10	33, 122
63:1–4	108
63:3	94
65	122
65:17	118

Jeremiah

51:36	119

Ezekiel

1–2	44, 58
1:1	59
1:5–14	62
1:22	61
2:8—3:3	83
2:9–10	64
2:10	64
26–28	102
28:13	127
37:27	78, 122
38–39	114
40–48	33, 84, 123
47:1	127
47:12	127

Daniel

1:12–16	49
2:28	40
7	45
7:2–3	119
7:4–8	90
7:7	98, 101
7:9	45
7:13	43
10	45
12:4	13, 129

SCRIPTURE INDEX

Hosea

1–3	107

Joel

2:10	75
2:31	75
3:13	94
3:15	75

Nahum

1:4	119
3:1–4	98

Zechariah

4:2–6	44
6:1–8	33, 73
12:10	43
14:7	121
14:11	121

PSEUDEPIGRAPHA

Apocalypse of Paul

21:24–28	59

2 Baruch

22:1	59
29:4	119

1 Enoch

10:4–5	111
10:11–12	111
14:15	59
60:7–8	119

100:3	94

4 Ezra

6:49–52	119

Testament of Levi

5:1	59

NEW TESTAMENT

Matthew

6:9–11	26
6:9–10	124
12:28	14
24:33	52

Luke

22:18	107

John

1:1	109
7:37–39	127

Romans

8:20–22	118

1 Corinthians

10:11	14
15	118

Ephesians

2:20–22	123n10
5:22–33	107

SCRIPTURE INDEX

1 Thessalonians

4:13–18	118

Hebrews

1:2	14

1 Peter

2:5	123n10

2 Peter

2:4	111

Jude

6	111

Revelation

1–3	59
1	30, 38, 56
1:1–3	2
1:1	2, 4, 20, 39–40, 59
1:3	2, 6, 8, 13, 30, 40–41, 59, 100, 131, 134
1:4–6	42, 128
1:4–5	8
1:4	2, 30, 43, 60
1:5–6	43, 60, 66–67
1:7	43
1:8	30, 43, 62
1:9–20	43
1:9–16	82
1:9	2
1:10–20	44, 47
1:10	21, 29, 44, 59, 98
1:11	29
1:12–16	30, 32
1:12–13	44
1:13	47
1:14–15	50
1:15	45
1:16	47, 52
1:17	30, 45, 131
1:18	45
1:19	45–46
1:20	32, 44–45, 85
2–3	7–9, 12, 29–32, 41, 44–46, 56–57, 66, 81, 84, 112, 135
2:2–3	48
2:7	31, 117
2:8–11	11, 98
2:9	53
2:10	61
2:11	117
2:13	47, 49
2:17	117
2:26–29	117
2:28	131
3:4–5	61
3:5	117
3:7–13	11
3:12	117
3:13	11
3:14–22	11, 98
3:17	55
3:18	61
3:21–22	61
3:21	59, 61, 117
4–22	12, 26, 46, 57
4:1—22:5	128

SCRIPTURE INDEX

4–5	17, 21, 24, 26–28, 57–59, 68–72, 77, 81, 90, 106, 124, 130, 141	6	24, 27, 72, 76, 78–79, 82
		6:1–17	29
		6:1–12	33
		6:1–8	73
4	59–60, 63–64, 66, 69, 71, 136, 140	6:1	72–73
		6:3–4	73
		6:5–6	73
4:1	57, 59, 108	6:7–8	73
4:2	21, 29, 98	6:9–11	11, 67, 75, 78
4:3	125	6:10	105, 110
4:4	61, 65	6:11	61, 77
4:5	21, 78	6:12–17	75
4:6–8	62	6:15–17	27
4:7	62	6:16–17	95
4:8	30, 62, 99	6:16	78
4:9–11	62, 69	6:17	75
4:10–11	61	7	27, 75–78, 82, 93
4:11	63, 68		
5	59, 64, 66, 69, 71–73, 82–83, 131, 140	7:1–8	22, 76
		7:1	62
		7:3	76, 91
5:1–7	66	7:9–17	76–77
5:1	64	7:9	30, 52
5:2	64, 66	7:11	77
5:3	68–69	7:15–17	77
5:4	65	8–9	33, 36, 53, 82, 85, 119
5:5	65, 76		
5:6	20–21, 65, 90	8	78
5:7	66–68	8:1–3	82
5:8–10	66–67	8:1	29, 72, 78
5:8	67	8:3–5	67
5:9	66	8:4	78, 82
5:10	30	8:5	61
5:11–12	66	8:6—9:21	29
5:12	68	8:7	79
5:13–15	62	8:8	79
5:13	66, 68–69	8:9	79
6–22	27	8:10–11	79
6–20	26–27	8:12	79
6–8	59	8:13	79–81, 86

SCRIPTURE INDEX

Revelation *(continued)*

9	86
9:1–11	25, 79–80
9:1–2	110
9:6	81
9:7–8	80
9:13–19	81
9:18	81
9:20–22	81
10–11	82
10:1—11:14	79
10:1—11:13	86
10	81
10:5	94
10:6–7	86
10:6	83
10:8–11	82
10:8	82
10:11	30
11	81–83, 87, 89, 98
11:1–13	82
11:1–2	83, 85
11:2	84, 87–88
11:3–12	22, 84
11:3–6	85
11:3	84, 87–88
11:7–10	23, 85
11:7	80, 87, 110
11:9–10	125
11:9	30
11:11–13	85
11:13	86, 126
11:14	86
11:15–19	28–29, 79, 81
11:15–18	86–87
11:15	86
11:16–18	86
11:17	30
11:19	61, 86
12–22	87
12:1—22:5	82
12–13	22, 25, 87, 92, 96, 110
12	16, 22, 25, 33, 49, 88–89, 114
12:1–6	88
12:1	87
12:5	87, 109
12:6	87–89
12:9	89
12:10–12	88
12:10	112
12:11	88
12:12	86
12:13–17	22
12:13–16	88
12:14	87, 89
12:17	89
13	5, 25, 85, 89, 92–93, 97–99, 101, 109, 114
13:1–10	90
13:1	5, 61, 119
13:2	90
13:3–4	90
13:3	90
13:5–10	90
13:5	87, 89
13:6–13	93
13:7–10	90
13:7	30, 125
13:9–10	11
13:11–18	90
13:16–18	91
13:18	35
14	28, 92–93
14:1	92
14:2	93
14:4	142
14:5	93

SCRIPTURE INDEX

14:6	30	17:7–18	98–99
14:7	126	17:7–8	99
14:9	92	17:9	98, 100
14:11	92	17:10	100
14:12	93	17:11	100
14:13	30	17:12–14	101
14:14–16	28, 93	17:12	101
14:17–20	28, 93	17:13	101
14:19	95	17:14	101
15–16	80, 119	17:15	30, 101, 125
15	94	17:16–18	101
15:1	94	17:17	102
15:3–4	95	17:18	85, 102
15:3	30	18	93, 98, 101–2, 105–6
15:4	126		
15:5–8	94	18:1–8	102
16–22	83	18:1–4	105
16	28–29, 33, 36, 53, 83, 95	18:1–3	102
		18:4–8	1–3
16:7	30	18:4	103, 116
16:8	30	18:5–7	103
16:12–16	107	18:6	103
16:13	90	18:7	103, 124
16:15	30	18:8	103
16:17–21	98	18:9–10	104
16:18–21	61	18:10	85
16:19	106	18:11–17	104
17–20	97	18:11	104
17:1—19:10	29	18:12–13	104
17–18	22, 25, 96–98, 106–7, 116, 122	18:16–17a	104
		18:16	85
		18:17–19	105
17	32, 98, 102	18:17b–19	104
17:1–6	98, 101, 103	18:18	85
17:1–3	107	18:19	85
17:1	98, 116, 125	18:21–24	105
17:3	21, 29, 98, 104	18:21	105
17:4–5	98	18:23	120
17:4	99, 124	18:24	105
17:5	99, 120	19–22	16, 30, 41, 139
17:6	99	19–21	29

SCRIPTURE INDEX

Revelation *(continued)*

19–20	25–26, 28, 80, 86, 96, 108, 110, 116 125
19	53, 110
19:1–10	106
19:1–3	106
19:1	106
19:3	106
19:4–5	106
19:4	62, 106
19:5–9	109
19:5	106
19:6–9	122
19:6–8	107
19:6	30, 106
19:7–9	55
19:8–9	52
19:8	61
19:9–10	107, 130
19:9	30
19:10	68
19:11–21	21, 52, 96–97, 107–8, 113–14
19:11–16	108
19:11	73, 107–8
19:12	109
19:13	108
19:14	109
19:15	50, 109, 125
19:16	109
19:17–21	125
19:17–18	109
19:19–21	23, 109
19:20	90
19:21	109
19:22	85
20–22	47, 117
20	109–110, 115
20:1–10	97
20:1–3	110–11
20:4–6	51, 55, 61, 68, 86, 110–11, 113–15, 117, 139
20:5	113–14
20:6	30
20:7–10	96, 110, 113, 125
20:8	114, 125
20:9	114
20:10	90
20:11–15	97, 110, 113
20:11	118
20:12	52
20:13	61, 119
20:14	49, 52, 113
20:15	115
21–22	26–28, 114, 141
21:1—22:5	22–23, 25–26, 29, 31, 50, 53, 77, 84, 86, 97, 113, 115, 117–19, 123, 128, 132–33, 140
21	68, 108, 116, 139
21:1–5	118
21:1–2	48
21:1	54, 61, 80, 118–19
21:1c	119
21:2	22, 122, 124
21:3	78, 122, 132
21:4	78, 119
21:5	55, 118
21:6	21, 30, 78, 127
21:8	49, 119
21:9–21	22, 33

SCRIPTURE INDEX

21:9–10	116	22:6–21	129
21:9	122	22:6–9	130
21:10	21, 29, 98, 122	22:6	2, 130, 132
21:11	60, 123–24, 126	22:7	6, 30, 100, 129, 131–32
21:12–14	61	22:8	2
21:12–13	122	22:9	68
21:14	122–23, 125	22:10	2, 6, 13, 129, 134
21:16	123	22:12	100, 129, 131
21:18	123–25	22:12a	131
21:19–20	125	22:12b	131
21:21	123, 125	22:13	30
21:22	30, 120	22:14	30, 131
21:23	120, 122, 126	22:15	132
21:24–26	23	22:16	130–32
21:24	125–26	22:17	129, 132
21:25	121	22:18–19	6, 41, 132
21:26	125	22:20	100, 129–30
21:27	119	22:21	8, 128, 132
22	75		
22:1–5	140		
22:1–2	127		
22:1	21, 78, 123–24, 127		
22:2	23, 31, 123, 125, 127, 132		
22:3–5	68, 78, 124		
22:3	121–22		
22:4–5	128		
22:4	128		
22:5	51, 57, 120–21, 124, 126, 128		

EARLY CHRISTIAN WRITINGS

Against Heresies

iv.14.1	2
v.30.3	2

Hist. Eccl.

3.39	2n2

www.ingramcontent.com/pod-product-compliance
Lightning Source LLC
Chambersburg PA
CBHW022120160426
43197CB00009B/1097